DISCOVERING HOPE

DISCOVERING HOPE

BUILDING VITALITY

IN RURAL CONGREGATIONS

DAVID POLING-GOLDENNE AND L. SHANNON JUNG

Augsburg Fortress

Minneapolis

DISCOVERING HOPE
Building Vitality in Rural Congregations

This book has a companion video, *Stories of Hope in Rural Congregations* (ISBN 6-0001-3326-X). Order from Augsburg Fortress by calling 800-328-4648.

Developed in cooperation with the Division for Congregational Ministries of the Evangelical Lutheran Church in America, David Poling-Goldenne, project leader.

Scripture quotations are from New Revised Standard Bible, copyright © 1989 Division of Christian Education of the National Council of the Churches of Christ in the United States of America. Used by permission.

Editors: Laurie J. Hanson, Andrea Lee Schieber, James Satter

Cover design by David Meyer
Text design by James Satter
Cover art copyright © 2001, PhotoDisc, Inc.
Illustrations by Brian Jensen, Studio Arts

ISBN 0-8066-4147-9

The paper used in this publication meets the minimum requirements of American National Standard for Information Sciences—Permanence of Paper for Printed Library Materials, ANSI Z329.48-1984.

Manufactured in the U.S.A.

Contents

Foreword

Bank presidents from across the United States gathered at a conference to study equal opportunity lending to ethnic minority people. A number of scholars addressed this issue, including sociologists, economists, and anthropologists. The presentations and content were excellent and of high quality. I shall never forget, however, the moment when one banker stood and simply said, "This is a wonderful conference, yet I do have one question: in spite of our failures—and they are real—we have many loan officers in our banks who are very good at lending to ethnic minority persons. Some of them have done so for years. Has anyone studied what our best practitioners in the banks are doing? Have we invited any of them to tell us what they do?"

It was a stunning comment and a perceptive question. Apparently, no one had even considered such a possibility. Instead they had turned first to the "experts," ignoring that there were some potential experts in their very midst. Without a doubt, there are many loan officers who are very good at what they do and have learned a great deal in their work with ethnic minority persons. Hearing from these practitioners could have greatly strengthened the impact of the conference.

It is delightful, therefore, to see this book on vitality in rural congregations. Poling-Goldenne and Jung reverse the process of the bankers' conference. While both of them are well informed about the lives of rural congregations and their people, what they have done here is to ferret out the best practices in exemplary rural congregations. Through the careful and involved process they report here, the leadership team guiding this study identified 26 of the most effective rural congregations and studied in detail the practices of these congregations in the areas of prayer, worship, discipleship, evangelism, congregational care, and leadership. I cannot think of a book more needed in the field of rural ministry. In fact, we need exactly such studies in every area of congregational research.

In recent years, attention has turned to the crucial role of practices in congregational life. It is difficult to exaggerate the importance of such an approach. We learn things through practice that simply are not available to us otherwise. For example, apart from "practicing prayer," there are things we will never know about it. Or, when people say you do not have to go to worship to be a Christian, it is always a sign that they have not significantly practiced worship in a community of faith. The turn to the practice-based church is an important move. At the same time, such practices do occur in a context. Here, Poling-Goldenne and Jung have placed us in the hands of rural leaders and congregations who practice effective ministry. This is a much needed and unusually wise guide for the rural church.

Tex Sample
Author of *U.S. Lifestyles and Mainline Churches*
and *The Spectacle of Worship in a Wired World*

Acknowledgments

M any thanks are offered to the people who have made this resource possible. First and foremost are the people and pastors of the rural congregations who responded to the invitation to participate in this research study. They gave countless hours meeting together, filling out questionnaires and capturing their story so that this resource might become a reality.

Special thanks also to the Lutheran Brotherhood Foundation for two generous grants made over a period of two years to support this project and gather participants from the teaching congregations.

Thanks also to Martin Smith of the ELCA Department for Research and Evaluation for support with statistics and research, to Andrea Lee Schieber, an editor with Augsburg Fortress, for championing this cause as a needed resource, and to Tex Sample, a master storyteller whose parables mirror the power of the Master Storyteller 2000 years ago, for the way he set the stage during the congregational Discovery Event and for his kind words prefacing this resource.

This work is dedicated in memory of Warren Sorteberg, a faithful servant of God who served the Evangelical Lutheran Church in America as an ordained pastor and through the Division for Outreach until his death in 2000. Warren was an early partner in shaping this project and a consistent voice in support for rural congregations and leaders.

To God be the honor and glory!

INTRODUCTION

Putting This Book to Work

Discovering Hope: Building Vitality in Rural Congregations is written for laity and clergy who are or may be doing ministry in rural settings. Through stories and examples, it identifies the best practices of exemplary and effective congregations serving in these contexts. These practices were identified in a research study, which is described in chapter 1 and the appendix.

Discovering Hope is divided into nine chapters. Each chapter ends with a workbook or discussion section, providing a brief Bible study and questions that help readers apply the content. This book is designed to be used in three different ways:

- As an individual reader.
- As a congregation group study resource.
- As a guide and content for a learning event that could be sponsored by your synod or judicatory.

Individual readers are encouraged to use the closing section of each chapter as a personal workbook. The greatest benefits from this resource may come to those using it as a group study resource. Participants in a group should each have their own copy of the book. Schedule monthly or weekly meetings. Or consider using this book as part of monthly ministry team or congregational council meetings. Invite participants to read one chapter in advance of each meeting. Use the materials provided at the end of each chapter to process your learning together at the meeting.

Leaders wishing to utilize this book in a learning event format or retreat setting will need to adapt the content in the ways that work best. Each participant might be encouraged to read the book prior to the event.

Definitions

Some definitions and qualifications are necessary to set the stage for your discovery in this book.

This book employs the word *practices* as a way to describe the core ideas, moves, and actions at the heart of the external, visible work a congregation does. Practices take the form of initiatives, activities, and programs that vary from one congregation to another. The practices discussed in this book represent core actions for health and vitality in rural congregations.

The words *effective* and *vital* are used regularly to describe the congregations that participated in the research study. These words are used to connote a sense of being alive, hopeful, and filled with God-given energy. *Effective* simply means it's working. Lives are touched and transformed. These congregations are thriving. Much like a thriving plant, they are showing growth and energy, in terms of worship attendance and discipleship ministries. However, to be effective is not simply to grow numerically. Although numerical growth is happening to a greater or lesser degree in all of the congregations studied in this project, this growth is a by-product of the winsome, engaging culture shaped by the practices lifted up in this book.

Obtaining *Discovering Hope* resources

Additional copies of *Discovering Hope: Building Vitality in Rural Congregations* (ISBN 0-8066-4147-9) can be ordered through Augsburg Fortress by calling 800-328-4648.

The companion video, *Stories of Hope in Rural Congregations* (ISBN 6-0001-3326-X), takes you on a "virtual visit" to the three congregations highlighted in Chapter One. This video also can be purchased through Augsburg Fortress.

CHAPTER 1

Stories of Hope:
Finding Vitality in
Rural America

"We had thought about closing. Our numbers were going down each year and it was getting harder and harder to meet our budget. It seemed like there were fewer young people in the congregation, and those who had grown up here went off to college and didn't come back."

"Each bad year for farming made it that much tougher for our congregation to make its budget. Finally it got to the point where it looked like we weren't going to make it."

"It would have been easy to just fold up our tent at that point. I remember the meeting where it came to a head. The council decided they had to put this before the congregation. Mr. Olmsted showed us the direction in which our finances were going. Then Mrs. Hanson got up and pointed to the confirmation pictures on the wall. In 1964 there had been 22 in the confirmation class. In 1984 there were 12. The year of this meeting, it didn't look like there would be a class at all. People's spirits got lower and lower."

"Finally Bob got up. We thought if Bob was going to pack it in, then there was no hope. But Bob surprised us all. 'You know,' he said, 'I feel as bad about all this as anyone. My grandfather was baptized at this church and my parents were married here. Things don't look good. But I figure, with God's help we've always got a chance. I'm just not sure we've really given God a chance here. Do we really think we've given God our best efforts?'"

From that point on, this congregation reports, a turnaround began to happen. This did not take place overnight, and not without some hard work and a lot of prayer. People in this congregation figured they had nothing left to lose. Doing things the conventional way had led to a gradual loss of energy. Now it was clearly a matter of turning everything over to God.

At this low point people began asking themselves some important questions:

1. What is the purpose of our church and what are its most essential activities?
2. What is the mission of our church?
3. How has God gifted us in some unique and special ways?
4. How do these gifts intersect with the needs in our community?

Welcome to a journey of discovery.

After much prayer, Bible study, and hard work, the congregation turned around. People in the congregation began to look outward and became more involved in the community. They took pride in making their church a welcoming place. Some older ways of doing things were dropped and some newer ways were embraced. Now, more than 10 years into the turnaround—yes, it does take time—this congregation is very much alive.

To be vital or to have vitality is to manifest life and possess energy, to be lively. This book tells the story of vital and effective congregations in rural settings. It is about discovering hope and building vitality in rural places, places that sometimes deal with hopelessness and great despair. It is a story about turnaround, about how congregations reinvent themselves and, through the direction of the Holy Spirit, claim new realities for their existence.

This is a story about God's heart for rural congregations and the power of the Holy Spirit to awaken new energy and build a renewed focus that results in congregations that grow in influence, numbers, and impact on people's lives. Welcome to a journey of discovery that may have significant implications for the ministry of your rural congregation.

Where's the hope in rural America?

"Lately, it seems hardly a day passes without some negative news about the current rural crisis. People are losing farms, crop prices are fluctuating, and big companies are controlling the field."

"Our town just isn't like it used to be. Things are kind of dead around here. Shops are closed up. Now we have to drive into the next major town over to buy our groceries, see the doctor, and go to school."

There is much despair in rural America. Rural crises and economic realities have made life tough. Poverty, loss, depression, addiction, and abuse occur with growing regularity in rural communities. A whole way of life is changing, so much so that in some places a sense of hopelessness spreads throughout the community.

Congregations in rural settings mirror their communities. That's to be expected. The economic and political realities of Monday through Saturday living cannot be left at the church door on Sunday mornings. Add to this the weight of comments like "We are too small," "We have no young people," and "We just can't afford our pastor," and there is a perfect recipe for hopelessness and despair. Many congregations in rural America find themselves stuck in the mud of this kind of thinking.

Is there hope for congregations in rural settings? This was the driving question behind the research study and this book. Are there rural congregations discovering hope and building vitality?

The good news is that there are! What if we could study these congregations and listen to their stories? What would we learn that might be worth sharing with others? Are there characteristics or practices common to these congregations that can be transferred to others who seek to be vital in their settings? The answer to all these questions is "yes." This book seeks to share discoveries about vital rural congregations in a way that will be helpful to others.

From the field for the field

What might it mean to identify effective congregations from a variety of rural settings and put their ministries under a microscope? What would be learned? What could be discovered?

The premise of this book is that the real experts on congregational vitality in rural settings are the people who have experienced it first hand.

In the autumn of 1998, more than 140 rural ELCA congregations were identified as exemplary following a nomination and statistical review process. ("Exemplary" meant they were thriving and showing some growth in worship attendance and discipleship ministries.) These 140 congregations received invitations to join a research study, along with an extensive questionnaire directed to clergy and lay leaders. Of those congregations, 49 responded with completed questionnaires. The leadership team for this study reviewed all applications thoroughly and drafted an initial summary document highlighting insights to be tested more fully at a Rural Discovery Event.

You will hear from the places and people who are effective in ministry in rural settings.

Afterward, 26 congregations from across the United States were invited into the second phase of the study. These 26 congregations convened local on-site Discovery Teams over the summer of 1999 to discuss their ministries and complete comprehensive "Study Guides" that were returned to the leadership team.

In September 1999, each of the 26 congregations sent representatives (one clergy member plus two lay leaders) to meet with the leadership team for a Discovery Event. The three-day Discovery Event was designed to celebrate the ministries of these congregations, gather participants in focus and affinity groups, and capture information and ideas. This book represents a comprehensive summary of the entire project. (Further information concerning the procedure of this research, including the names of the participating congregations and members of the leadership team, can be found in the appendix on pages 117-124).

It is from the rich, fertile soil of this information, representing hundreds of pages of feedback from questionnaires, Discovery Guides, and the Discovery Event, that the stories and the best practices highlighted in this book have emerged. Although this study focused on ELCA rural congregations, the information gleaned here is more than applicable to most mainline rural congregations.

As a result, in this book you will hear from the places and people who are effective in ministry in rural settings. You will learn from the ones with the calluses on their hands and the dirt under their nails just how they have answered God's call to vital ministry. The best practices discussed here are from the field (from those who have done it and are doing it), for the field (for those in similar contexts willing to learn from their colleagues and partners in ministry).

The changing face of rural America

Ask a dozen people to share their definition of *rural* and you are likely to get a dozen different answers. The fact of the matter is that what constitutes *rural* is changing in North America. The old stereotype of the white church with a steeple surrounded by wheat or cornfields is just one picture of a rural setting today. Rural congregations are now found in agricultural, mining, logging, ranching, open-plain, recreation, and small-town settings—or any combination of the above—in just about every state in this nation. Stop and take a moment to notice the diversity of the congregations that participated in this research project (see the appendix at the back of this book). These congregations demonstrate that there is no typical rural context. You will certainly need to define what rural means to you in your context.

In "What Happened to the Farmers?" (*Net Results,* November/ December 2000), Lyle Schaller, a highly respected consultant and observer of congregational trends, comments on the significant changes that have taken place in rural America over the last century. As Schaller notes, a few years ago the U.S. Census Bureau decided to no longer tabulate data specifically on farmers for the following reasons:

1. The number of farmers in the United States had shrunk so much that there no longer was any point in counting them.

2. Most people living on farms are not active farmers.

3. Most people working on farms do not live on those farms.

Consider these statistics in the same article: "Between 1920 and 1941, the farm population in the United States fluctuated between 30 and 32 million . . . . By 1990, the total was 4.6 million people, one-seventh the number of the 1930s. As some people left their farms, others moved into rural America. Thus the total rural population increased slowly from 54.5 million in 1950 to 59.5 million in 1980 to 61.7 million in 1990. The rural nonfarm population experienced the big increase from 27 million in 1920 to 44 million in 1970 to 57 million in 1990."

When translating these trends, Schaller writes, "In 1940, farming-community churches across America had a combined potential constituency of 30 million farmers and their families, plus a rural nonfarm population of 27 million. Sixty years later those churches have a combined potential constituency of fewer than 4 million farmers and their families, plus a rural nonfarm population of 58 million. Several million of the current rural nonfarm population, however, are really urbanites who combine country living with commuting 15 to 50 miles each way to a city paycheck. Many of them find it easy to commute 'only' 10 to 15 miles to shop, go to the movies, see a doctor, go to school, visit friends, or go to church."

These trends explain why so many rural congregations find themselves in transition. As population shifts, communication venues—such as TV and the Internet—become more available and global, and schools continue to offer a more standard, universalized curriculum, people in the pews become less distinct and more alike. Congregations often find themselves caught between the way life was "back then" and the growing needs of the present population.

Rural settings vary from place to place, which leads to the question, Can *rural* be used to describe context? One of the better discussions of this topic can be found in the book *Rural Congregation Studies: A Guide for Good Shepherds* (L. Shannon Jung and Mary A. Agria, Abingdon Press, 1998). Jung and Agria argue that there are some "common qualities of 'ruralness' that can be extrapolated from [a variety of the above mentioned] settings; qualities that affect the life of parishioners and hence the role of pastors" (p. 30). Jung and Agria offer a matrix of four categories that can be helpful in understanding why people identify their own context as rural:

Geography and demographics
- The community size and population density.
- The potential for greater intimacy.
- The potential for isolation.

Economy
- Land-centeredness; the extractive focus (on things taken from, grown from, fed by the land) of the economy; infrastructure struggles (e.g., closing schools, limited retail, etc.) that are a result of a sparse tax and population base.
- Dependence, in many cases, on a single, primary industry.

Population characteristics
- Stable population over time.
- Power tending to issue from a core of longtime or lifelong residents.

Mind-set or values
- Tradition (the status quo) valued more than innovation.
- Life roles (work, leisure) more integrated and wholistic.
- "Land" as a factor in people's identities and lives.
- *Experience* and *time* perceived more as cyclical than linear.
- Less value placed on introspection or self-analysis, since custom (e.g., habit, ritual) is accepted as the best state of being.

Chances are that if any number of these qualities are part of your context and your story, you are fairly comfortable in identifying your setting as rural.

Rural congregations in the ELCA

Rural congregations represent more than half of the congregations in the Evangelical Lutheran Church in America (ELCA). This means that the health and vitality of these congregations is of primary importance to the church as a whole. Rural congregations matter! They are the church!

Rural congregations matter! They are the church!

Of the 10,825 congregations in the ELCA, 3,329 grew 5% or more in average worship attendance between 1995 and 1999. Of these growing congregations, 17.9% were in rural farming areas, 6.7% were in rural, non-farming areas, and 18.7% were in small towns with populations of less than 10,000. This represents a total of 43.3% of the congregations that saw growth in worship attendance. There is vitality and strength in rural congregations! The diversity in the sizes of rural congregations in the ELCA is also interesting to note:

34.5%	175 baptized members or less
30.7%	176-350 members
14.4%	351-500 members
9.2%	501-700 members
5.9%	701-950 members
5.3%	more than 950 members

There is great diversity in rural congregations. Consider the following statistics gathered by the ELCA' Office of the Secretary in 1999:

- 24.1% of all ELCA congregations are in rural, farming areas.
- 6.2% are in rural, non-farming areas.
- 20.8% are in small towns with populations of less than 10,000.
- 51.1% (the above three categories) or 5,088 congregations are in settings with populations of less than 10,000.
- 1,765,700 people or 35.9% of the ELCA's baptized membership is in these congregations.
- These congregations contributed $37,714,342 in benevolence or mission support, representing 30.3% of the ELCA's total.
- Of the 5,088 congregations, 3,172 (62.4%) are located in zip code areas that grew from 1990 to 1999; 1,890 were in declining zip codes; 21 in zip codes with a stable population.

Projections through 2004 suggest: 3,157 (62.1%) of these congregations are located in zip-code areas that will increase in population between 1999 and 2004; 1,900 will be in declining zip-code areas, with 26 in zip codes with a stable population. (Statistics for this section were compiled by the ELCA Department for Research and Evaluation.)

The verdict? There is power, hope, and great potential in rural congregations!

Three stories to set the stage

Meet three congregations from three distinct settings: 1) in an open country farming context; 2) a two-point parish in which the town congregation serves as a gathering place for the surrounding county; and 3) a smaller town congregation that has survived conflict. Three different locations, yet one similar story.

These congregations have come alive through the power of the Holy Spirit. They have reinvented themselves for effective ministry. They are making a difference in people's lives. These are just three of the dozens of stories that could be told. Let them set the stage for your discovery of the practices that make for effective ministry in rural settings.

These three congregations are featured in the companion video for this book, *Stories of Hope in Rural Congregations*. The video can be a helpful discussion starter for the workbook section of this first chapter.

East Lake Andes Lutheran Church,
Lake Andes, South Dakota

At East Lakes Andes Lutheran Church in South Dakota, there is a small but growing community filled with spirit and changing lives. Now the community is vital and growing, but things weren't always that way. In fact, there was a time when some thought this congregation was on its last legs. Not any more. Refusing to cave in to despair, East Lake Andes took some simple but powerful steps to bring new life to the community.

Drop into East Lake Andes on a Saturday morning these days and you're likely to find farmers gathering for a rural crisis and support group meeting. They share, network, and pray at these meetings. Drop in during planting season, and you'll see tractors, combines, trucks, and people pull up to the church to invoke God's blessings on their life and work as part of the Rogation Sunday celebration. Pop in some Sunday during worship, and you might find the pastor on her guitar and the congregation singing a playful, home-grown song celebrating their context.

There is power, hope, and great potential in rural congregations!

The Farm Song

(sung to the tune of "If I Were a Butterfly")

If I were a white Charolais, I'd thank you Lord,
For giving me hay.
And if I were a Hereford cow, I'd thank you, Lord,
For showing me how.
If I were a curly haired sheep, I'd jiggle my tail
And I'd give you a bleat, but . . .
I just thank you Father for making me "me."

(chorus from "If I Were a Butterfly")

If I were a Case-I.H., I'd thank you Lord,
For giving me fuel.
If I were a green John Deere,
I'd be thankful for my power-shift gears.
And if I were an old, blue Ford, I'd finish my work
And I'd take on more, but . . .
I just thank you Father for making me "me."

(chorus from "If I Were a Butterfly")

If I were a flower bed, I'd thank you Lord,
For my blooming stems.
And if I were a garden plot, it's tough to be
Thankful for the bugs and whatnot.
And as I mow my lawn I'll say,
"It's a lot like farming, in a city way," but . . .
I just thank you Father for making me "me."

You might even find several members proudly wearing shirts with the word TOUCH printed on the back. The word stands for the congregation's mission statement: Teach God's word, Outreach the gospel, Uplift others through fellowship, Care about the needs of others, and Honor God through creative worship.

East Lake Andes is in the open country, surrounded by growing fields. The congregation is growing, too, through creative, vital worship; effective, meaningful teaching; and dedicated, relevant service. A new building addition recently was completed. This faith community, which eats breakfast together each Sunday morning, looks for ongoing ways to serve the larger community with crisis support and childcare. The church that some thought might close is now blowing with the fresh wind of the Holy Spirit.

Zion Lutheran Church, Cobleskill, New York

Pop over to Zion Lutheran Church in Cobleskill and you'll find a congregation more than 200 years old, right in the center of town in this service-oriented rural area. It's obvious from Zion's location that it has held significant influence for the town and surrounding community.

The church itself looks right out of the picture books: a red brick building, beautiful stained glass windows, and a high steeple tower with a cross. A walk through the assembly hall takes you deep into the congregation's history with a display of historic items and a wall of photos of the 37 pastors who have served Zion over the years.

More than 20 years ago, some people wondered if Zion's season of significance was past. Worship and Sunday school attendance had decreased and the budget could not be met. In the winter, worship services were held downstairs in the assembly hall to save on heating costs.

Drop in now, and you can feel the Holy Spirit working. You can sense vitality and mission and renewed energy. How did things turn around at Zion? This turnaround is not due to some significant evangelism program or special campaign. It has emerged over the last 20 years as a result of a renewed intentional focus on prayer and Bible study. Zion's pastor is a patient, caring leader. He believes with a passion that Jesus is God's answer in a need-filled world, and models the power of prayer, calls his people to pray, and gathers them through Bible study and small groups into a revival that is spreading into the community.

St. John Lutheran Church, Nashua, Iowa

Visit in Nashau and what you'll find is a clean rural town with friendly people. This is a middle-class, blue-collar community that was once predominantly elderly, but has seen a number of young families move in during the last few years.

At St. John Lutheran Church in Nashua, you'll find a 100-year-old congregation with a German background, a congregation that has had its ups and downs, most recently surviving a conflict involving a former pastor: "In the past we were considered a cold, exclusive church and residents did not want to be a part of us. Within the last five years, however, we have come full circle. We are now a growing friendly congregation that reaches out to the unchurched. We offer a warm atmosphere, an excellent Christian education program, and uncompromising biblical truths."

We are now a growing friendly congregation that reaches out to the unchurched.

The pastor of this congregation summarizes the feel of this place when he writes: "Jesus told us to make disciples of all nations. We passionately believe that knowing and having a personal relationship with Jesus Christ is absolutely essential for every person in the world, so we try to do whatever it takes to bring people to Christ and help them become his disciples. So, for example, we offer a variety of worship styles and times during the week so more people will be able to come and hear the Good News. We offer a family-based confirmation program to encourage connections between parents and their children. And we actively support a food pantry and a mission partnership with a redeveloping congregation in another community."

The following chapters in this book highlight the best practices discovered in exemplary rural congregations throughout the research study. Borrowing another congregation's activities or programs is not a recipe for long-term success, but in the stories and examples you will find principles, ideas, and models that have worked in rural settings. You can adapt and apply these practices in your congregation, taking into account your history, resources, needs, and context. Applying the best practices in this way can unleash energy that will transform the life of your congregation. In the words of Jesus, who modeled best the power of stories to change lives: "Let anyone with ears listen!" (Matthew 11:15).

Taking it home

Use the following material on your own or as part of a congregational planning group. The Bible study and questions serve as a launching point for personal or group discovery concerning the best practices modeled by effective rural congregations.

Individual or group Bible study

Read John 4:3-42, the story of Jesus' caring ministry with the woman at the well in rural Samaria. Pay particular attention to verses 34-38. As you read, imagine the context and reflect on the nature of the relationships in this community. Picture the setting and the drama of this story. Then, on your own or as a group, reflect on the following questions:

1. What is the rural context for this story? How does Jesus speak to the context through his words and actions?

2. Describe the character of this community as you surmise it from the story: What are the issues and human dynamics?

3. What does this story suggest about rural ministry and rural evangelism strategies?

Setting the stage for future discovery

Individually or as a group, reflect on the three congregations' stories offered at the end of chapter 1. If you have the companion video, you may wish to view or show the video at this point. Reflect on the following questions:

1. What strikes you as most interesting or notable in the three stories and why?

2. What appear to be the practices or dynamics behind the turn-arounds these congregations experienced? Make a list based on your reading or viewing.

3. Think about your own congregation. Are there similarities between your situation and these three congregations? How is God breathing vitality into your congregation's life?

4. Discuss insights gleaned from your reading of the earlier content in chapter 1. What is your context for ministry? Are you comfortable defining yourself as *rural*? How have the changes suggested by Lyle Schaller impacted your congregation? Does the information shared about rural congregations in the ELCA trigger any reactions or thoughts for you?

CHAPTER 2

Prayer:
Letting Go and Letting God

 *Practice:* Effective rural congregations are spiritually alert, regular, and intentional in their prayer life and activity. They seek Jesus' power, guidance, and direction in their planning and ministry.

> *"Five years ago we were an at-risk church. We decided to pray and study Scripture. We were led to build a new church. Our attendance went from 40 to 160. People are now comfortable using the name of Jesus. Our mission is to reach people with Jesus. This transformation has been what has welcomed other people in."*

These words were spoken with passion, as if to communicate that this was the critical key to unlocking the door to turnaround and vitality in a rural, recreation, and commuter-oriented congregation in Verona, New York. When leaders in the congregation got serious about mission in their setting, they didn't quickly engage a set of ministry activities. First, they prayed! They prayed and studied the Bible; they listened, let go, and ultimately let God guide and direct their ministry focus and priorities. This was and continues to be the key to their transformation.

It is no coincidence that this book begins with prayer and spirituality as the first practice modeled by effective rural congregations. Through each phase of our research study on growing rural congregations, the practice of prayer rose to the surface as the critical piece to the ministry transformation puzzle. Congregations might effectively model every other best practice, but it is clear that if a God-centered focus brought alive through active prayer is not present, healthy growth simply does not happen. Prayer is the way these congregations tap into the holy, discern God's will for their ministry, and find the energy to embrace the mission opportunities that surround them.

Letting God be God

The psalmist captured a truth reflected in the experiences of most vital and effective rural congregations. These congregations discovered, sometimes accidentally, sometimes out of the desperation of ministry circumstances gone bad, and other times through intentional Bible study, that "Unless the LORD builds the house, those who build it labor in vain" (Psalm 127:1). A key to congregational turnaround, it seems, is getting out of the way: inviting God deep into the planning and conversation process, seeking God's insight, will, and guidance in all facets of the ministry.

In congregations that demonstrate vitality, prayer is seen as the conduit to harnessing God's power and intent.

Getting in touch and in tune with God happens through prayer: public prayer as a gathered community in worship and small groups, and focused individual prayer among the key leaders and members of the congregation. In congregations that demonstrate vitality, prayer is seen as the conduit to harnessing God's power and intent. It is the glue that binds

Leaders in one rural, northern-California congregation explain what drives their ministry focus: "We want people to experience a personal encounter with Jesus."

They read Scripture with the expectation that God will speak to them. Their prayers and devotions are quite particular and pointed— they expect to hear God addressing them. What is most remarkable about this congregation's worship and prayer life is the expectation

that Jesus is calling them to particular actions and ministry today.

They ask, "How can we communicate Jesus, even as we long for Jesus?" So these church members pray regularly for opportunities to witness to Jesus in their daily lives.

A lay leader from this congregation said, "I was blessed by being able to bring Christ to work with me." This is the spirit that permeates this place due, in large part, to the regular practice of prayer.

members one to another in these faith communities. It is the fuel behind the congregations' evangelism efforts; indeed, it powers their mission focus and the passion to reach their neighbors. God becomes real, tangible, and expressible through the regular practice of prayer. Lives are touched, changed, and transformed inside and outside the congregation as a result. These congregations have discovered that power is unleashed through the practice of prayer, because God is out and about doing ministry in and through them for the sake of others in their communities.

Spiritual alertness

These congregations are serious about seeking God's will for the work they are called to do.

"You can hear it in their language, their choice of words," a research project leader commented while comparing two sets of focus groups with rural congregations in Nebraska and Wisconsin. Focus groups were convened in each state: one, with numerically growing congregations in demographically stable or growing settings and another, with congregations declining in worship attendance in the very same demographic context. The same questions were asked in each group, and the results were striking: participants from growing congregations talked about God and the Holy Spirit; those in declining congregations didn't talk about God at all. In fact, there was little to distinguish declining congregations from the local civic group or community club.

This revelation can't be overstated. Effective rural congregations know Jesus, talk about Jesus, and see God acting in and through their ministry. Their language and behavior acknowledge the presence of God in their midst, guiding and shaping their choices. People in these congregations speak of Jesus as friend, brother, mentor, and guide. They are spiritually alert, unafraid and unashamed to drop the name of Jesus. Pastors and lay leaders employ God-talk in their decision-making and conversation about ministry. They also refer to the Holy Spirit and regularly use faith language.

Prayer drives the vision and mission

"We were just begging for the Lord to guide us in appropriate ways. The scary thing is that when you do sense that you might have a grasp of God's vision, you start to think, 'Oh my, is this really what God is about here?'"

Notice the way God figured into the conversation as three lay members (**A**, **B**, and **C**) of a town congregation in New York and a rural congregation in Winchester, Virginia, talked about pastors:

A: They have an authentic relationship with God. They are very much aware of this relationship and it is very important to them. So it is easy for them to see how it could be important for others as well. From the inside out, they are excited about Jesus and the difference he makes in their own life and what that can do for the lives of others.

B: A lifestyle that reflects servant-hood, Jesus' practice of humility.

C: Motivating, not in the sense of fine language, but more in the sense of the kind of life they lead. You are eager to follow, appreciate the joy of being around and following along with that person.

A: You can say they have a "passion" for God and they can see the Holy Spirit working.

C: They experience blessing, and people get built up in their own faith walk.

Comments like this one, spoken by a congregational leader in Virginia, typify the way effective rural congregations seek God's guidance and inspiration in their vision planning and ministry. These congregations are serious about seeking God's will for the work they are called to do. They pray with expectation, confident that God will give them the direction they need. They seek to be about God's agenda, not their own.

"Everything starts with prayer," a leader from upper New York said, "Everything starts with prayer and is grounded in Christ, and then we end that way. That's what gives our compass bearing." So it is not unusual in these congregations for committees and ministry teams to spend up to one-third of their time in prayer and study. Every meeting or gathering in the congregation begins with prayer: prayer that acknowledges God's presence; highlights that the congregation is in mission and has a mission; and more times than not, reminds all the people gathered that they exist to serve their neighbors, not just themselves. The leadership teams—congregation council or board of elders, for example—see themselves less as decision makers driven by budgets and the choice of the

Through a time of study and prayer, God made clear to the leaders of an upstate New York congregation (quoted in the opening story of this chapter) that they needed to move to a more visible ministry site and rebuild their house of worship.

In the time of preparation for building, this congregation did an amazing thing to seek God's guidance and to provide a witness to the community. They erected a prayer tent at the site of their new building and scheduled 40 days of prayer, during which members and interested folks from the community came to discern God's will for the congregation.

This highly visible expression of the congregation's intent to be God-driven in their focus has had a significant effect in attracting the surrounding community to the church. There are many new faces. Less tangible, but no less real, is the spiritual energy unleashed in this congregation through prayer.

paint color in the restroom, and more as vision casters and prayer leaders about the task of discerning God's will. A leader from New York shared, "There needs to be that constant prayer. Holding it up to the Lord, saying, 'Help us, Lord. Show us. What do we do next?' Then listening. Then things begin to fall into place."

In many cases, when these congregations pursued their own agendas, ministry bogged down, conflicts erupted, and life together was a burden. However, when God's will is sought and attended to, good things happen, joy abounds, and a spirit of energy and vitality arises. The other fascinating discovery is that when this shift in orientation occurs, it almost always turns these congregations from an inward focus on themselves as "family" to a desire to meet, greet, and serve those who are not yet a part of a faith family. Simply stated, prayer sets the stage for evangelism.

Praying at all times

Prayer is the heartbeat in effective rural congregations. It is constantly practiced, preached, modeled, and taught. Pastors are seen to be the chief pray-ers, but only in the sense that they provide the modeling and momentum to regularly remind members of the importance and power of prayer. These congregations look for opportunities to teach others how to pray, and they are particularly intentional about this with their youth and children. One congregation leader from Wyoming, in reflecting on her work with youth, said, "It's amazing what 15 minutes of prayer with these kids is doing. It's amazing what they are praying about. Who knows what the unchurched kids are taking home to their families."

A peek into the spiritual lives and practices of these congregations reveals a host of common and not-so-common prayer ventures: prayer chains; intercessory prayer groups; prayer vigils; prayer retreats; distribution of prayer packets and devotional materials to members; prayer before meetings, choir practices, and study groups; heartfelt, free-form prayer during worship, often also lay led; anointment for healing as a regular part of communion services; e-mail prayer and devotions delivered by the pastor to members at home and work; intentional prayers for others by youth within their meetings and gatherings; mentor relationships pairing veteran, seasoned members with youth and children for the sake of prayer and encouragement; and more.

Prayer is the heartbeat in effective rural congregations.

Perhaps the story that best illustrates the spirit of all this prayer activity is from Zion Lutheran, a town congregation in Cobleskill, New York. Wanting to model and teach prayer, leaders made the simple move of seeking verbal prayer requests during the worship service. This doesn't happen through hastily written pew cards or even at the beginning of the service during announcements. Instead, after the sermon is preached and

---

One congregation went so far as to call forth a "Spiritual Growth Team" whose primary purpose was to plan spiritual activities and retreats for all ages.

One outcome of this effort is an intercessory prayer group that schedules at least one person to be in church praying one hour each day for the needs of the congregation and community. Cards are sent out to all the people who have been in the congregation's prayers.

The effect is tremendous. The Spiritual Growth Team also created a prayer labyrinth walk as a physical way to model the importance of prayer.

just before the prayers of the church, the worship leader pauses and invites worshipers to share their requests out loud. At first the invitation was met with reluctance, but over time a new perspective emerged in this place: "People express these things out loud and understand that they might not even be included in the exact prayer time, but God is listening while we are sharing and it becomes a way of encouraging openness about the needs and concerns of the congregation, as well as the joys."

At Maynard Wang Lutheran Parish, a two-point parish in rural south-western Minnesota, the pastor invited a 90-year-old shut-in with a gift for drawing to create confirmation folders for the youth in the congregation. As a result of this effort, the woman took on the commitment to pray regularly for each of these teens. She is a "prayer warrior" of the congregation even in her physical absence from the gathered community.

Prayer works!

It is clear, and needs to be unequivocally stated again: Prayer is a crucial ingredient for effectiveness in congregational mission and ministry. Without a strong focus on prayer, a congregation will not be truly transformed. A praying church is a vital church. A vital church is a church meeting the needs of its members and a church in mission to its neighbors.

Best practices for vital ministry

Prayer is a crucial ingredient for effectiveness in congregational mission and ministry.

Effective and vital rural congregations demonstrate the following best practices for prayer:

1. *Prayer is central.* Members and leaders of these congregations pray regularly and intentionally. They teach prayer, model prayer, and expect God to act through prayer.

2. *Prayer provides their marching orders.* These congregations have learned that vitality comes from getting out of the way and letting God into the picture. As they tap into God's vision for their ministry, the energy released is winsome, engaging, and attractive.

3. *Prayer is practiced in dozens of creative ways.* From a prayer chain to a prayer tent, these congregations aren't afraid to try new ways to tap into the spiritual power to be effective in ministry.

Taking it home

Use the following material on your own or as part of a congregation planning group to maximize your understanding of this practice and to discover what you are already doing well, what you might consider strengthening or initiating as a result of your learning.

Individual or group Bible study

Read Luke 11:1-13. By this time in Luke's gospel, the disciples have experienced numerous miracles and healings. Chapter 10 of Luke tells how 70 people were sent in pairs to "every town and place" to cure the sick and proclaim the closeness of God's reign in Jesus. That chapter concludes with Jesus gently correcting a busy and preoccupied Martha with the words: "Martha, Martha, you are worried and distracted by many things; there is need of only one thing. Mary has chosen the better part" (verses 41-42). Note the marked shift in the first verses of chapter 11. "He [Jesus] was praying in a certain place, and after he had finished, one of his disciples said to him, 'Lord, teach us to pray' " Some of Jesus' most well-known words follow: the Lord's prayer and two illustrations about God's desire to hear and answer prayer. Reflect on the priority and practice of prayer in your congregation.

A praying church is a vital church. A vital church is a church meeting the needs of its members and a church in mission to its neighbors.

1. In what ways has your congregation gotten "worried and distracted by many things"? How is the busy-ness of ministry in your setting similar to what the disciples may have experienced in their walk with Jesus?

2. Does your reflection on this particular chapter move you to ask, "Lord, teach us to pray?" What might it mean to go the way of Mary and choose "the better part"?

3. How might the Lord's Prayer provide a model for renewal in your congregation's prayer life and focus? How can you apply Jesus' further teaching about prayer (Luke 11:5-13) to the circumstances of your congregation?

Celebrating present strengths and ministry

An honest evaluation of your congregation's current life of prayer can help you determine how to grow forward in your prayer ministry. The following page includes a self-evaluation from the book *Growing Your Congregation's Prayer Ministries,* by Brent Dahlseng.

Take a moment now to assess the present value prayer receives in the life of your congregation. Evaluate each item below on a scale of 0–10 using this key:

0–2 = very seldom   3–5 = seldom   6–7 = often   8–10 = almost always

To determine your average score, total all of the scores and then divide by 10.

_____ Prayer is understood as a key part of our pastor's job description.

_____ Prayer is a daily expectation for leaders of our congregation (council or board members; heads of committees or teams).

_____ Prayer is seen as critical to the faithful preaching of God's word and worship leadership.

_____ Prayer seminars are offered one to two times a year; at least 10% of our congregation's members attend annually.

_____ Prayer opportunities are available for the congregation and community during the week.

_____ Prayer partners pray for our congregation's staff and their families.

_____ Prayer articles and references appear consistently in our congregational communications (newsletter, bulletin, Web page).

_____ A Prayer Room is available in our church building and is used by members.

_____ Prayer is available before or after worship through the ministry of a prayer team.

The self-evaluation on pages 34-35 originally appeared in the book *Growing Your Congregation's Prayer Ministries,* by Brent Dahlseng (Chicago: ELCA Division for Congregational Ministries, 1998). Used by permission.

_____ Answers to prayer are made known in the congregation to thank God and inspire faithful praying.

Few congregations will consistently score in the 8-10 range. Look at your scores and identify your strengths and build in those areas of perceived weakness. Look for creative ways to build an active practice of prayer within your congregation.

Two action steps

Based on your reading, reflection and conversation, name two activities you might consider implementing over the next six months to a year. Keep them manageable and achievable. Select ideas that will maximize the practice of prayer in your community of faith.

CHAPTER 3

Worship: Building Community and Hope

Practice: Effective rural congregations provide vital and vibrant worship experiences that celebrate the mystery of the extraordinary in the midst of the ordinary, cast a vision of hope and meaningful discipleship, sometimes even in the face of hopelessness, and build a sense of family and community in places where there can be loneliness and isolation.

> *"Do you know what draws people to your congregation?" The question was simple, but the response was profound for its implications. "There is joy and hope in this place," responded an eager member of a vital, rural congregation in South Dakota. "People come because it feels like 'family.' They come in comfortable clothes. The pastor is warm and available. We have fun in church. We laugh in church."*

In effective rural congregations, worship is a high priority for the people's life together. Worship is considered to be critically important, and great care is taken to do it well. It is the primary time when the congregation gathers as "family" to honor God through praise and song, to seek God's guidance for daily life through God's word read and applied, to pray for the needs of others, and to carry out faith through action and service. But it is also much more.

Story after story reveals that there is something more than the content of the worship experience that ensures its power and vitality. It is essential that the "spirit" of the congregation is warm, family-like, informal, spontaneous, relational, and fun. Members of vital congregations often talk of an energy that is infectious, a spirit that is contagious, a sense of awareness and expectation that the Holy Spirit is present and very much a part of their worship encounters.

Done well and with feeling

Inspiring worship in rural congregations comes in a wide variety of styles with a wide variety of sounds. Almost all of the congregations in the research study offer worship services patterned on the rubrics of their denomination's primary hymnal, but often with a great deal of freedom in the choices of liturgy and song. Several congregations provide contemporary worship services or blended service options, utilizing a more informal presentation style, free form prayers and a praise band or simple ensemble. Two incorporate country western music in their worship. One, seeking to be relevant to its Hispanic neighbors, offers bilingual worship and Spanish songs.

The truth is, these congregations don't have all the pieces often associated with church growth and vitality. They don't all have services designed specifically for newcomers; however, most are oriented to the newcomers in their midst. They don't all have great music, wonderful choirs, or talented liturgists. What they have, it seems, is "spirit." They have vibrant, creative, energetic worship that speaks to the needs of the people who gather in their community, that utilizes the available resources in their midst and is experienced as genuine and God-shaped by those who gather to experience it. The key is neither style nor content, but instead doing whatever they do well and with feeling.

Reflecting on what attracts people to her rural church, a lay leader from northern Wisconsin said, "Good solid worship . . . and variety. People actually come for what the church is primarily known for. Its worship services!" A lay leader from Minnesota added, "Sing songs people can sing; the biggest sin of Lutherans is boring hymns."

The pastor from a town congregation in New York commented on the importance of worship that connects:

"A stale worship experience week after week needs to be shaken up. In the past, one of our most ineffective models of evangelism was doing the service by the book and assuming people just knew the liturgy. We found that visitors didn't return, despite the friendliness of the congregation. They didn't come back because the worship service didn't connect. . . . We found a way to offer choices and issue a wake up call."

Preplanned and creative

The focus is on helping people experience the presence of God through their worship together.

For the most part, in these growing congregations worship is carefully thought through and planned out in advance. Seldom is worship pieced together at the last minute or done by the book as if the hymnal were a cookie-cutter recipe that simply needs to "walked through." This is not to suggest however, that there isn't room left for spontaneity or the in-breaking of the Holy Spirit. Indeed, the focus is on helping people experience the presence of God through their worship together. This often is done by ensuring all the elements hold together thematically and usually involves intentional coordination between worship planners and leaders.

In rural congregations, pastors are the primary worship leaders. They may gather some key lay leaders to assist, but it is clear the vision for worship and most of the planning responsibility resides with the pastor. For the most part, pastors of vital and effective congregations place highest priority on their role as worship leader and preacher. They understand worship to be the primary gathering for the community and spend a good amount of time carefully planning their congregation's worship experiences.

Many of these pastors, while still clearly assuming the lead, intentionally mentor and train lay leaders to assist in worship planning and leadership. In fact, the greatest vitality exists in places where worship truly is the work of the people, ranging from the more familiar roles of lectors and worship assistants, to lay preachers and the offering of regular testimonies in worship at one congregation in northern California. It is clear, however, that the pastors continually work at identifying and calling forth leaders. Without that vision and drive, lay leaders are not likely to assume significant roles. The only exceptions to this are in some places with pastoral vacancies or in multi-point parishes, where lay leaders appear to step forward more intentionally on their own.

Talk to them, not at them

"What is it about your church that attracts outsiders?" Without blinking, a lay member from a town congregation in east-central Wisconsin responded, "The pastor's sermons, the worship experience! People feel as if they are being talked to, not talked at."

Worship leaders in effective rural congregations regularly find ways to help worshipers experience the extraordinary in midst of the ordinary. They don't hit home runs every week, but for the most part, worshipers speak of regularly experiencing the call and presence of God through worship in a way that impacts their daily life: their choices, relationships, work, and families.

While music, drama, and liturgy are all part of how this occurs, it happens most consistently in the pastor's preaching. In the questionnaire phase of the research study, dozens of references to the importance, power, and value of the worship message suggest that this may be the most important venue for helping worshipers experience God in their lives and for leading them to be effective disciples. This is not because other venues, such as Bible study and small group experiences, don't work. They do, and the impact is often quicker and goes deeper. However, worship is the time when the greatest number of people gather for Christian education.

Sermons are used to teach and motivate people to embrace their walk with Jesus. Great care is taken to relate God's story, to make the Bible come alive in a way that speaks to the daily lives of the gathered people. Some pastors regularly feel freedom to depart from assigned lectionary texts to create message series that are thematic and speak to the particular struggles and needs of the people in their community. There often is no assumption that worshipers know the Bible well and care is taken to help people make the connections.

Worship leaders in effective rural congregations regularly find ways to help worshipers experience the extraordinary in midst of the ordinary.

Some pastors view the worship time as one of basic catechesis—moments during which the basics of the Christian faith are shared in ways that make sense and apply to the daily realities of their people. There almost always is great sensitivity to context. In a rural farming community, stories of the earth and crops abound. The economic stresses of farm life are addressed. The joys, cycles, and struggles of agricultural life shape the message. In a town context, issues of work, school, stress, and commuting give color to the spoken word. In a rural mining or ranching context, the stories and hurts of those occupations flavor the message.

Finally, and this, from all reports, appears most important: the pastor is perceived as genuine, caring, and transparent. Pastors disclose their own personal journeys, share their human foibles, and regularly communicate that they are on a journey toward deeper discipleship themselves. The worshipers see that this is serious stuff which the pastor lives and believes, and that it really is a matter of utmost importance for everyone to pattern their lives in this way as much as, with God's help, is possible. At East Lake Andes Lutheran Church, Lake Andes, South Dakota, each worship service begins with a time for sharing personal concerns and prayer requests. It is not uncommon for this time to stretch from 10 to 15 minutes.

Light a candle whether or not it's dark

"Our agricultural community is private and stressed; the economy is affecting the whole community. Our worship is a place of hope. We need to make a place for hope."

It would not be an overstatement to say that vital and effective rural congregations are like lighthouses of hope in their communities. They are safe, secure harbors where people find support, friends, and community. Their worship services are places where the hurts and fears of everyday life are addressed and where an alternate reality is lifted up and proclaimed. Through worship, participants often find themselves lifted in spirit and encouraged for their journey. Beyond this spiritual support, people also find the value of "a family" of friends who assist them physically and even financially. Good news in these congregations extends beyond the preached word. It is made visible in a caring community that lives out discipleship by helping fellow members and others.

Creating hope appears to be a major priority, whether or not leaders of the congregation intentionally plan for it. Worship services are inspiring and light, relational and warm. Messages are filled with more gospel than law. Christ is lifted up as a friend who walks alongside and bears people's daily burdens.

Creating hope appears to be a major priority.

Welcome all

During the focus-group phase of the research study, a lay leader from New York caused heads to bob affirmatively by saying, "People are not looking for a friendly church. They are looking for friends."

One of the strong suits of effective rural congregations is that they build community: they become "family" to those who are searching for connections and friends. Although feelings of loneliness and isolation are not exclusive to rural communities, in effective rural congregations, people are welcomed, befriended, and incorporated with great ease. These congregations know people are hungry for community. They know people can find a place and a home in their midst. And most importantly, they are open and eager to welcome others to the family.

The stage for this hospitality and welcome most often is set in worship. Through the preaching and teaching, members are encouraged to be open and invite others. A number of congregations provide for regularly scheduled "Bring a Friend to Worship" Sundays. Others find creative ways to welcome children in worship, even to the point where one Wisconsin congregation provides a regular kids' church. Another congregation has the youth lead worship once a month. Another has a sixth-grader play piano for worship as a way to mentor new leadership and communicate that the community is open and inclusive. A lay member from Spooner, Wisconsin, reflected on the significance of worship. She said, "Worship is like a battery charger for us . . . a constant source of revitalization."

For the ease of guests, in several congregations the entire worship service is printed out in the bulletin, if not every week, certainly for times like Easter, Christmas, and confirmation. One congregation in upper New York instituted a "three minute rule" and promoted the idea in the newsletter and through announcements. Each Sunday, as part of the benediction, the worship assistant proclaims: "Go in peace . . . and remember the three minute rule," which is the signal that members should talk to people they don't already know for at least three minutes.

Give them Jesus

As Jesus is shared and experienced in the midst of the ordinary, hope is cast and community is built.

There was a time when many people thought the small-town congregation at Trinity Lutheran Church in Salem, Ohio, would have to close its doors. A handful of long-time members, remembering the glory of days long gone, didn't have the funds or the energy to make things work anymore. A new pastor was called to redevelop the congregation, some said to give it one last chance.

Perseverance, patient teaching, casting a vision, teaching, prayer, Bible study, and leadership development contributed to the turnaround in this congregation. Surprisingly enough, much of this took place through the congregation's worship services.

It's important to know that this is a congregation that once worshiped by the book. There was a time when walking into its worship space felt like stepping back into the 19th century, and kids were rarely seen in worship. But much of that has changed. The following experience symbolizes the shift and freedom this congregation now practices in its worship life.

About eight years into the turnaround, the house was full, and the pastor had just finished preaching when a six-year-old girl got out of her pew, came forward and tugged at the pastor's robe: "Can I sing? . . . I've got something I want to sing for everybody." What could the pastor do? After all, she had been encouraging spontaneity, the use of gifts, and the importance of being attentive to God's Spirit, but this wasn't the right time. So the pastor said, "Sure, when we are finished with communion."

After communion, the pastor called the girl forward, announcing that the girl had something to share. Not sure what the girl was going to do, the pastor handed her the microphone. With the confidence of Broadway star, the girl let forth the most beautiful rendition of "Jesus Loves Me." There wasn't a dry eye in the house. The symbolic power of that young girl's witness didn't escape the pastor or the congregation. The reason for their turnaround was Jesus; their focus on Jesus, their worship of Jesus, their prayers to Jesus, their intentional study of Jesus' word, their intentional seeking of Jesus' will, and their growing awareness and confidence that indeed, Jesus loves them.

Worship in growing rural congregations leads with Jesus. As Jesus is shared and experienced in the midst of the ordinary, hope is cast and community is built. This kind of worship definitely is a factor in congregational growth and vitality.

Best practices for vital ministry

Effective and vital rural congregations demonstrate the following best practices for worship:

1. Worship is highly honored. Worship is seen as the time when the largest number of members gathers to honor God, grow in their discipleship, and discern God's will for their collective and personal lives. Leaders expend intentional effort and energy in making worship the best that it can be within the realities and limits of their setting.

2. Worship is relevant to the context and the needs of the gathered community. The language, style, music, and forms of worship are sensitive to the people who gather to honor God in their space. Care is taken to craft a worship experience that connects with people's hurts, hopes, and lives.

3. Worship is flexible and creative. These congregations break out of the box to keep worship interesting and vital. This happens most frequently through the use of contemporary and praise music and through creative presentation of the Word.

4. Worship services are seen as times to build hope and create community. The predominant focus is on building people up, encouraging hope, and strengthening the ties of support and friendship among members and the people in the community.

Taking it home

Use the following material on your own or as part of a congregational planning group to maximize your understanding of this practice and to discover what you are already doing well, what you might consider strengthening or initiating as a result of your learning.

Individual or group Bible study

Read Luke 9:28-36, the story of Jesus' transfiguration on the mountain. Peter, John, and James were treated to the worship experience of a lifetime. This dramatic experience had Jesus at its center and it was a confirmation of his person, power, and ministry. It was tempting to revel in the worship moment. But Jesus moved Peter, John, and James through the encounter to the benediction and sending. They were to leave the mountain in order to serve and heal in the valley.

Read the questions on the following page to reflect on your congregation's worship life.

1. What parallels or differences can you identify between your personal story and the story of the transfiguration?

2. Based on your reading of this chapter, which of the four worship highlights are illustrated within both the story of the transfiguration and your congregation's own experiences?

3. Pick five adjectives or phrases you might use to describe the worship practice and tone in your congregation. What do these choices communicate about worship in your congregation? If you are working in a group, share your thoughts with each other. Note similarities and differences. What can you celebrate as blessings and identify as growing edges?

Celebrating present strengths and ministry

Use the following list to assess your congregation's present worship practice in light of the discoveries highlighted within this chapter. Mark each phrase with "A" (already part of our common practice), "C" (could be strengthened as part of our common practice), or "D" (definitely need to pay attention to this in planning). If you are working in a group, share your thoughts with each other. Note areas to celebrate. Highlight those ideas that merit further consideration.

____ Worship is a high priority and is done well.

____ People sense that there is a high investment of energy and time in planning worship services.

_____ Worship is perceived as vital, relevant, and meaningful most of the time by most of the people.

_____ Visitors and guests feel at home during worship services and often return for worship again.

_____ People speak of a sense of "spirit" in the congregation that can't be easily captured in words.

_____ Worship services are open to spontaneity and surprise.

_____ For the most part, people feel comfortable expressing themselves in worship through song, spoken prayer, applause, testimony, and so forth.

_____ Sermons are easy to understand, using concepts and illustrations that connect with people's lives, occupations, and needs.

_____ Many people are involved in leading worship, especially youth and children.

_____ Worship builds community and a sense of hope among most worshipers most of the time.

Two action steps

Based on your reading, reflection, and conversation, name two activities you might consider implementing over the next six months to a year. Keep them manageable and achievable. Select ideas that will maximize the value of the worship life in your congregation.

CHAPTER 4

Making Disciples: Learning to Live Jesus' Way

Practice: Effective rural congregations encourage people to join the adventure and journey of discipleship by creating a culture in which Bible study and devotional reflection are central. Learning to follow Jesus with one's whole heart, mind, and body is the aim. The teaching focus, while certainly content-based, aims more at equipping adults, youth, and children to live a lifestyle that is Christ's style.

> *"Let the word of Christ dwell in you richly as you teach and admonish one another with all wisdom, and as you sing psalms, hymns and spiritual songs with gratitude in your hearts to God. And whatever you do, whether in word or deed, do it all in the name of the Lord Jesus, giving thanks to God the Father through him" (Colossians 3:16-17).*

Paul's words to the church in Colossae powerfully summarize a core value in effective rural congregations: people of all ages, in age appropriate ways, are regularly encouraged to "let the word of Christ dwell in you richly" in order that they might come to know Jesus and discern God's will and way for their individual and collective lives. These congregations encourage and teach growth in discipleship using all of the means available to them in their settings, from the ordinary to the creative, to animate their people to a faith walk that is active, relational, and lifelong.

When asked, "What is your definition of discipleship?" pastors and lay leaders responded with these comments:

- "Always learning, never arrived."
- "The process of following Christ in every aspect of life."

- "Starting a sixth-grader playing the piano for the congregation."
- "Trying to live as Jesus lived."

Jump-starting a discipleship culture

It needs to be said early on. Discipleship had not always been a priority in most of the congregations invited into the research study. In fact, most of the pastors and lay leaders talked of a time, not more than a few years ago, when the spiritual life of the congregation could be characterized as arid and desert-like. Ministry had its bright spots then, and certainly lives were touched through Bible study, confirmation, and other education ministries, but this was done rather mechanically and with little enthusiasm or conviction.

To make disciples, one must first be a disciple.

It also needs to be said that in most of these congregations, people still feel they are jump-starting a discipleship orientation in their settings. They have not arrived, and would be the first to say that they are experimenting, learning, and growing as they go. Nevertheless, it is clear that turning up the temperature on Bible study, learning, and discipleship has been key to the turnaround and revitalization of these congregations.

A number of the vital rural congregations studied are more than 60 years in age. Over time, they have reinvented themselves several times. In these places, the key to the latest revival is a renewed focus on teaching and making disciples.

Disciples make disciples

Jump-starting a discipleship focus in a congregation is not unlike turning over a near empty or dead battery in car. The battery must be connected to a power source that is running and fully charged. To make disciples, one must first be a disciple.

Pastors often cast the vision and create the momentum for a discipleship focus, and are dedicated and passionate disciples themselves. They will be the first to acknowledge they are not perfect, however, as they working at being faithful themselves. They study scripture regularly and aspire to maintain a disciplined prayer life. Their lives, actions, and demeanor model, as much as humanly possible, a Christ-like walk.

These pastors appear to be transparent about their faith walk—they talk about what they do, model it regularly, and take time to highlight the benefits of living a faith-filled life. They cast an invitation to discipleship that is more caught than taught. Because of their words and actions, others aspire to emulate and follow.

For almost every congregation in this study, conflict was part of the turnaround process.

While pastors have a significant role in shaping this culture, clearly it doesn't necessarily begin or end with the pastors. Indeed, in each of these settings, lay leaders carry the vision deep into the congregation. The enthusiasm of lay leaders for faith and active discipleship is modeled through their own walk, their role as teachers, and their work on congregational committees and teams. While these leaders may be present in a congregation, members can also be nurtured to take on this role.

Strategies for building enthusiasm and ownership for a discipleship focus include distributing devotionals or Bible-reading plans to encourage regular Bible reading and prayer, holding retreats with hand-picked leaders, making Bible study and prayer times part of committee and board meetings, intentionally inviting selected members to Bible study, teaching about spiritual gifts and baptismal calling, and initiating a small group ministry focus.

The key is to "keep it open," shared the pastor from a rural tourism and recreation oriented congregation in Durango, Colorado. "Keep people growing wherever they are coming from. . . . It is like swimming. When the water is cold, jump in together, and it's much easier."

When asked, "What keeps people in your congregation participating in nurturing their faith?" a lay leader from a congregation in Cobleskill, New York, replied: "It's a discovery. They hear the good news and want to hear more. It's feeding them and filling them; then they want to continue."

The pastor from the same congregation was asked, "How is your congregation transforming members into disciples?" The answer: "We have been encouraging daily Bible reading. Several times we have encouraged people to read through the whole Bible in a year. That really helps to deepen faith. People want to live lives that are biblical."

One congregation in this study went so far as to vote on this. Leaders and members worked together to create a vision that calls for focused discipleship. They brought this vision to the congregation's annual meeting for a vote, and now print that vision on every bulletin, meeting agenda, and newsletter. This intentionality has gone a long way in

We try hard to communicate that discipleship is the expectation of the gospel. We don't shy away from the expectation. It is not an option. We try to get away from sounding legalistic, but at the same time we must embrace the opportunity to be of service and discover the excitement of Christian formation. It is so easy in congregations to make everything we do an option. We want to have folks willingly decide to be involved in activities of Christian formation, but there comes a time when the congregation has to take a stand and lead members by saying these are expectations."
—*Pastor from Bethel Lutheran Church in the town of Winchester, Virginia*

encouraging leaders to take up the cause and cross of discipleship in their settings.

In the small town of Buffalo, Wyoming, the expectation at St. Luke's Lutheran Church is that a member must be in a Bible study to serve on the congregation's council. The congregation's emphasis on Bible study and discipleship has led seven lay leaders, men and women ranging in age from twenty-one to sixty-nine years old, to preach before the congregation.

Not without conflict

Jesus' call to discipleship met with resistance in his day. The "we've never done it this way before" syndrome surfaces when congregations reorient themselves in ministry. Calling people to deeper discipleship can challenge people's comfort levels and complacency. Encouraging people to follow Jesus' lead means those who think they should have power will rear their heads.

For almost every congregation in this study, conflict was part of the turnaround process. In a focus-group discussion, a few lay leaders openly shared that sometimes congregations could only move forward with new health and growth when a few people left or were invited to find new faith communities where they could be happier. However, patient perseverance, a centered biblical focus, and intentional care by pastors and lay leaders usually carry a congregation through the turbulence.

At St. Luke's Lutheran Church in Buffalo, Wyoming, learning regularly takes shape outside of classroom walls. At the leadership of the pastor's wife, the congregation began an after-school program called "Angels Among Us" for children in first through sixth-grade children. Each Wednesday, children gather to play, learn, and practice songs they sing as a choir in the church and at nursing homes and community events.

During a recent Christmas season, the Angels went door-to-door with adults from the congregation to collect food for Christmas baskets for the neediest in the community. When they knocked on one member's door for donations, it was apparent that this particular family was having a rough time themselves. On the spot, the group created a basket from the offerings previously gathered. Faith is shaped in many meaningful ways through this not-so-traditional program.

"Discipling": A verb, not a noun

These congregations see themselves as greenhouses for making and sending disciples

Forming and shaping faith is clearly active and relational in effective and vital congregations. The intent is to make disciples who live as disciples, not just to pour a body of knowledge into a learner's head. While there definitely is an interest in teaching the basics of the Christian faith, this is done so that the knowledge will be expressed in changed lives of witness and service. These congregations see themselves as greenhouses for making and sending disciples. Their role is to nurture faith, grow it, give people opportunities to express it, and ultimately to encourage people to plant it in others so that the process continues. This is done within the context of community: people living and growing together in a mutual process of discovery and encouragement, discerning Christ's will and way for their lives.

Education ministry in these congregations is therefore more than Sunday school, adult forums, or Bible study. It happens through worship and preaching, through social ministry and action, through kids' clubs and camping ministries, through committee meetings, prayer groups, and even choir rehearsals. These venues become the fertile fields in which faith is incubated, fed, grown, and practiced.

From cradle to grave

Leaders and members of effective congregations promote the notion that learning and discipleship are lifelong processes. They regularly dismiss assumptions that learning is just for children and completed by the time one is an adult. They dedicate resources and energy to reaching everyone in the congregation, in age-appropriate ways, with the challenge to grow in faith.

The message is that learning and discipleship are fun!

Equipping adults to lead and serve

Adult faith formation is a high priority in these places because adults who become passionate about their faith become the best leaders in the congregation and community and the best teachers of others. "Do you want a vital Sunday school?" quipped one leader. "Then make discipling adults your priority; they'll take care of discipling their families and the children of the congregation." "We are building an expectation that adults will go deeper, attend Bible study, and be regular in prayer," shared the pastor from Zion Lutheran Church in Cobleskill, New York. This congregation promotes learning through regular Sunday classes and Bible studies, and by offering Alpha courses to the congregation and community.

At Immanuel Lutheran Church in Everson, Washington, adults of the congregation recently were asked to prioritize their lives from a scriptural perspective. For one year, every group in the church was invited to focus on the question "What does it mean to be a disciple?"

Two-month sessions and weekend workshops were offered throughout the year, utilizing pre-selected studies and resources. Spiritual formation groups covenanted to meet together on a weekly basis. The effect on people's lives is astounding! Besides introducing people to spiritual disciplines, this process enabled members to grow in their faith and practice.

"It gave me a small group to identify with, to share my faith story with, to disclose something of myself to," reported one participant. Another participant shared that this discipleship process had helped him "to cease the idolatry of having his hopes tied to the health of the economy."

(Alpha is a 12-week disciple-making program geared to new Christians.) Another congregation in the research study offers three regular Bible studies and has a healthy percentage of adults in the congregation enrolled in a chapter-a-day Bible reading program. One congregation has an adult forum so "vibrant, it meets through the summer even when Sunday school stops."

The sermon is perhaps the most powerful venue for teaching discipleship.

It is interesting to note some of the not-so-traditional offerings discovered in these congregations. One congregation has the Wild Women's Group. At St. Andrew's Lutheran Church in New York, a unique form of discipleship takes place in the "Brewer's Guild" where men share their lives and faith as they brew and sip homemade beer. One Wisconsin congregation offers a weekly study called "Heart and Soul," combining aerobics and Bible study. The message is that learning and discipleship are fun!

How are adults discipled most effectively? Five key strategies emerge from the congregations in the research study: through worship; small groups; retreats; participation in discipleship experiences sponsored ecumenically or by judicatories; and by focusing on spiritual gifts.

The sermon is perhaps the most powerful venue for teaching discipleship. Pastors in vital and effective rural congregations continually look for ways to use sermons to encourage and admonish their people to an active Christian walk. They offer sermon series on discipleship, provide clear examples of how to live and serve, and effectively apply scriptural principles to daily life.

The importance of small groups as the fertile field where faith grows is also clear. The use of small groups ranges from Sunday adult forums to

Back about eight years ago, there were several of us who were stay-at-home moms. Pastor saw that and identified a list of six people. He sent us all a letter and asked one of the young moms if she would be the leader. We got together and for several years we met as a small group for Bible study. This was an important time for learning and support."—*Lay member from Cobleskill, New York*

Bible studies and topical groups to intentional learning and prayer time with committees and choirs. "Small group experiences led by lay leaders in homes has made the biggest difference for us," shared one lay leader from Idaho. "This has become for us a primary evangelism strategy." Not all of the congregations studied have an intentional small-group focus like the congregation just mentioned, but they all stress the importance of gathering in smaller groupings for learning and nurture and found ways to provide those gatherings on a regular basis.

Retreats for key leaders provide powerful opportunities to focus time and energy on discipleship. "Retreats are extremely helpful and inspiring," said a pastor from Plymouth, Wisconsin. "We feel you get a new vision of Christian community and mission through these kinds of times. We come away energized and bring back lots of new ideas." Retreats in these congregations cover the gamut from council and leadership team building, to parenting and marriage, to intergenerational family camps, to spiritual discovery and prayer.

A number of congregations also actively encourage members to participate in discipling experiences outside of their faith communities. These experiences include events sponsored by the synod or judicatory as well as ecumenical offerings such as Via de Cristo, Alpha courses, community Bible studies, and retreats coordinated by outdoor ministry centers. One congregation even provides funds to encourage leaders to participate in such events.

A final strategy for making disciples is an intentional focus on spiritual gifts. Through the use of inventories and intentional teaching moments, members are regularly helped to discern their God-given gifts and encouraged to apply them in ministry both inside and outside the congregation.

Discipling children and youth

While adult education clearly is important in these congregations, the emphasis on discipling youth and children should not be overlooked. When congregations in the research study were asked to prioritize some items that described their discipleship focus, again and again highest priority was given to the statement: "We place a strong emphasis on discipling children and youth in standard and not so conventional ways

Our Sunday school and vacation-Bible-school programs are fun. The teachers are encouraged to be creative, and they are. We have an active youth Sunday school class. They often take responsibility for leading worship when the pastor is gone."
—*from the rural congregation of East Lake Andes Lutheran Church, South Dakota*

In Spooner, Wisconsin, puppet ministry is the talk of the town. "Our puppet ministry is a success," shares one of the pastors of this town-centered, regional congregation in rural northern Wisconsin. "Young people are competing to become a part of it. They are starting to write the scripts and take over the teaching of the younger children. This ministry is such a draw because the puppets use basic language, address the lives of the children, and use the kind of music this audience appreciates."

(for example, Sunday school, but also kids' clubs, summer day-camp ministry, and intergenerational learning options)."

In effective rural congregations, learning is active and inter-generational.

Learning is fun and adventurous in effective rural congregations. It is not seen as an option, but rather as an integral part of what is done as a follower of Jesus. Many congregations report that children can't wait to participate in their relational, creative learning activities. In fact, their focus on children is often a key to both their evangelism appeal and growth in the community. These congregations become important places for people to gather in hope-filled, caring communities. As friends invite friends, not only do parents in these congregations participate more eagerly, children in the community find their way into the congregation as well. And of course, these children often bring their families.

Portland Lutheran Parish is a unique faith community composed of six churches that have come together as one parish in the agriculturally oriented region of Portland, North Dakota. The parish is noteworthy in its strong emphasis on Christian education for youth, helping youth become "doers of the Word." Youth are involved in servant events, mission trips, worship, drama, and in caring for their community. Vacation Bible school is not held in a church building, but at the local high school.

Taking learning into the community in this way has helped to welcome others in.

Generations building community together

In effective rural congregations, learning is active and intergenerational. Instead of segregating groups by age, the faith community learns and grows together. It is not uncommon to see older adults and young children or youth and parents working and learning together. This multigenerational focus is evident in worship, special learning activities, servant events, and even in the committee or leadership structure of the congregations. At Ixonia in Wisconsin and Zion Hill in Pennsylvania, children and youth are integral players in outreach projects and in teaching ministries including Sunday school, confirmation, and youth groups as well as "moms and tots" groups and cradle roll ministries.

Strategies for discipling youth and children range from the traditional to the creative and not-so-conventional. There is attention to the basics: Sunday school and vacation Bible school (sometimes combining grade levels due to the size of the congregation), confirmation (sometimes done in partnership or ecumenically, due again to the size and needs of the context), cradle roll and nursery (sometimes overseen by one eager leader), and youth activities (often open to the community). There are also creative efforts clearly targeted to meet the needs of the wider community: nursery and day care, after school kids' clubs, summer day camp, off site meals, and Bible studies at schools, servant events, and mission trips.

"In your face"

Effective rural congregations find creative ways to continually remind people of their call to discipleship. They work at it and are strategic about it. They are consistently "in the face" of their members with the invitation and opportunities to go deeper in their walk with Jesus. At Bethlehem Lutheran Church in Sturbridge, Massachusetts, this happens through daily e-mail devotions sent by the pastor to interested members, devotions that lead up to and set the stage for the coming Sunday's sermon.

Effective rural congregations find creative ways to continually remind people of their call to discipleship.

At Bethel Lutheran Church in Winchester, Virginia, people are reminded of the call to discipleship through the regular use of a resource center library with Christian children's books and videos. This library is rolled right into the narthex each week, with the encouragement that youth check out resources on their own. This congregation also uses a Sunday bulletin insert which worshipers are encouraged to take home and use for table conversation and prayer during the week. These weekly inserts carry the themes from worship and education into homes as families gather together to talk about and apply what they have learned.

Vital and effective congregations have many more creative ways to promote learning and discipleship. They cannot all be listed here but it is clear that these congregations get people excited about the adventure and journey of discipleship.

Best practices for vital ministry

Effective and vital rural congregations demonstrate the following best practices for discipling:

1. *Place top priority on Jesus and his call to discipleship.* These congregations see the Bible as their primary curriculum and find creative ways to awaken people to the adventure and journey of lifelong discipleship.

2. *Take the long view in discipling.* Effective congregations recognize that learning is active, relational, and lifelong, and they strive to meet the needs of all ages. They invest in their future by training youth in the Christian life, devoting significant time and effort to their children, and exhibiting a deep love for youth. They encourage adults on the journey toward deeper discipleship, where discipleship is not something to be achieved once and for all, but something that is part of living the Christian life. Effective congregations take joy in this. They laugh and joke about it and are anything but somber Christians. People in these congregations are comfortable enough to work with each other, even when they disagree.

3. *Help youth and adults live their faith by encouraging them to take on significant roles in the congregation and community.* Youth and adults are expected to get involved in significant acts of service inside and outside the church. A mix of programs offers recreation, learning, growth, service, and action.

4. Create a sense of fellowship that supports the focus on long-term discipling. In effective congregations, there is a high level of caring for one another and friendships develop even across generations. This sense of family builds communities in which discipleship is a joy instead of a duty.

Taking it home

Use the following material on your own or as part of a congregation planning group to maximize your understanding of this practice and to discover what you are already doing well and what you might consider strengthening or initiating as a result of your learning.

Individual or group Bible study

The apostle Paul was a powerful teacher who labored tirelessly to form faith in new believers. Throughout his letters to churches, Paul highlights the need for growth in faith. Read the following passages from Paul's letters, noting what they communicate about the process of forming faith: Romans 12:1-2; Galatians 4:19-20; and Ephesians 4:11-16.

1. What images of faith formation are offered through these selections from Paul's writings?

2. How does your congregation labor tirelessly to form faith?

3. Which insights from Paul could be applied in your congregation?

Celebrating present strengths and ministry

Dozens of ideas and strategies for making disciples were highlighted within this chapter on discipleship. Engage in the following process to maximize your learning and move toward an action plan.

Step 1: Working either individually or as a group, go back through this chapter and write down as many ideas and strategies for making disciples as you can find. Record and post your observations so all can see.

Step 2: Make a list of key insights gained from your reading. What did you learn about discipling that you want to pay attention to? Record and post these observations.

Step 3: Make a list of discipling activities already going on in your congregation. What can you celebrate? Note where there might be room for improvement. Record and post your observations for this step.

Step 4: Review your lists from each of the previous steps and discuss the implications. What new ministries might you consider in your place? How might you turn up the temperature on discipling in your congregation?

Two action steps

Based on your reading, reflection, and conversation, name two activities you might consider implementing over the next six months to a year. Keep them manageable and achievable. Select the ideas that will maximize the practice of making disciples in your congregation.

CHAPTER 5

Evangelism:
A Way of Life

Practice: Effective rural congregations exhibit a holistic approach to evangelism built on relationships, centered around events, and focused on meeting the specific needs of people in the community.

"Our evangelism committee meets every Sunday morning at 8:30 and 10:00 a.m." This was the quick, tongue-in-cheek response when a leader of a rural congregation was asked about evangelism. This statement reveals much about the way effective and vital congregations approach evangelism.

"How does your congregation do evangelism?" In the research study, this question often drew blank stares. A number of congregations didn't have evangelism committees or working groups. Some of them were even proud of this fact. Several of the leaders revealed they didn't much like or appreciate the word *evangelism*.

And yet it was clear evangelism permeates almost every aspect of ministry in these congregations. Evangelism is practiced and lived out in dozens of tangible and creative ways and is indeed a factor in the vitality and attractiveness of these congregations. Here evangelism is often unplanned in the formal committee-driven sense. It is considered very much the work of the people, and is expressed foremost through the primary worship experiences in these congregations: "We don't have an evangelism committee. It just happens. We like to think this is the responsibility of everyone to reach out to others. On a Sunday morning, if there are visitors, members just don't say, 'Well, I'm not really on the evangelism committee, so I really don't have to speak to these folks.' We know it's the responsibility of all of our members."

Not a program, a way of life

If evangelism is defined as everything people do to reach and engage those who are not part of a Christian community with the invitation to come and live a life of discipleship and commitment to Christ, then evangelism is very much at the heart of ministry for these congregations. It is how they are wired in orientation to the people in their community.

For the people in these congregations, the motivation for reaching out to others is Jesus.

For the people in these congregations, the motivation for reaching out to others is Jesus. Sparked by a strong sense of the power of Jesus in their own lives and in the life of their congregation as community, they live knowing they have good news to share. They feel compelled to share with others their experience of this "community," the belonging they feel in Christ, and the sense of community they feel in the congregation. More often than not, the evangelistic invitation is first to the church, to an activity, an event, a worship service, or a small group gathering. But make no mistake, while it starts with an event or gathering, at the bottom line the invitation is always ultimately to Jesus.

When leaders of thriving rural congregations were asked which Bible verse best captures their sense of mission, Matthew 28:18-20 was the passage chosen most often. It is no overstatement to say that these congregations follow the Great Commission in its fullest sense of meaning. They model a holistic balance between a focus on mission (Go) and the faith formation (make disciples) of their present members and those they hope to reach. Reaching their neighbors is always ultimately for the sake of building disciples, transforming lives, and enhancing caring, Christian community.

This evangelism focus, however, is seldom programmatic or committee-driven in its planning and execution. In fact, many of the congregations do not have formal evangelism committees or planning processes. Evangelism is seen to be integral to every aspect of the congregation's ministry: "It is intentional that we do not have an evangelism committee, because we make sure that all the committees or ministry teams have an element of evangelism in everything they do from social ministry to Christian education and even property. For example, 'How does our property convey a sense of welcome?'"

How do these congregations manage to develop such a strong evangelism mind-set and practice without a formal structure or planning process consistently in place? It is clear that the pastor is key. The pastor is the chief evangelist, but not necessarily the primary and most effective inviter. In these congregations, the pastor is constantly and intentionally training, encouraging, and modeling an evangelism perspective. Through worship, preaching, teaching, and coaching, the pastor builds an understanding that Christ invites—that as Christ's modern-day disciples members are expected to invite, and that the congregation is going to do whatever it can to make it easier for members to invite. Although lay leaders cast this vision in some of the congregations, pastors who lead with a Great Commission heart and mindset are key to keeping members primed to invite, welcome, and receive new members.

An evangelism grounded in relationships

Not one of the congregations in the research study reported going door-to-door proselytizing. Instead, the focus is on helping the people of the congregation to invite others from within their natural webs of relationships: their friends, relatives, neighbors, and business and school associates.

When one member of a town and country congregation learned that several musicians in the area wanted to get together in some way, he brought this need before the church council. The congregation responded by developing "Sunday in the park" worship services and music events and inviting all in the community. These worship services are followed by lunch together, then musicians from the congregation and community continue to play long into the afternoon. These events build new relationships and provide a wider public witness to the community.

In a rural Wisconsin congregation, the community needed recreation and sports for adults. A group of congregation members decided to host a volleyball team in the faltering community league. Within two years, the congregation was fielding two teams and several new families had become a part of the congregation's worship life.

Effective rural congregations look at people's needs first (the need for community, the need to make a difference, and the need to connect with others) and then follow with content or program. In the midst of this exchange, the congregations know and expect that people will meet Jesus. It is as if the "congregation as place or community" becomes the evangelist. These congregations model a community warmth that is characterized by laughter, informality, and a sense of homecoming and welcome. Once a person experiences this community warmth, they are likely to want to return, become part of the congregation themselves, and know Jesus.

Evangelism focused on invitation

Evangelism in effective rural congregations could be described as "come and see." The emphasis is on invitation, a broad invitation targeted to the neighboring community in ways that are relevant to the context and a narrower and more productive invitation of friends inviting friends to experience the congregational community.

Broader community invitation strategies typically alert residents to the congregation's presence and value within the community and create an awareness that this is a place or a people worth checking out. These efforts make the congregation's face public, building a sense within the community that this is a place where some primary needs can be met. Effective rural congregations are creative in getting the word out in ways that take advantage of natural communication venues in the community.

Members of Bethlehem in Sturbridge, Massachusetts, are equipped to invite friends, relatives, and neighbors with business cards from the church. Each member is invited to carry the business cards and use them as invitations whenever opportunities present themselves.

The congregation also makes effective use of Christmas and Easter ads. To supplement these ads, members are encouraged to distribute seasonal invitation cards that list worship service times and location as well as the congregation's Web site address.

The people of Grace Lutheran in Mountain Home, Idaho, know that in their community an effective billboard can attract ongoing attention. They invest in a bright, eye-catching sign on the local highway.

The words on this sign always begin with "Grace is the place for . . ." The sentence is completed with a different word each month. "Fellowship," "joy," "worship," "belonging," "seconds," and "fun" have all been featured.

While the regular exchange of words on the billboard keeps the community looking and guessing, it also helps to build an awareness of the kind of community this congregation intends to be.

Examples include regular use of a village billboard, radio ads, distribution of brochures by youth to neighbors, special mailings to new neighbors, neighborhood newsletters, ads in local newspapers, and congregational presence at local civic events (such as parades or craft displays). The reality is that rural congregations have clearer paths of communication to their communities than do congregations in larger, more diffuse markets. Vital rural congregations communicate a great deal to their neighbors through consistent, regular press and their presence in the community.

A more effective way that these congregations engage evangelism is by encouraging members to invite their friends, relatives, neighbors, and associates to personally come and see. The congregations encourage this kind of invitation by sponsoring special activities or events (see the following sections for fuller detail). Whatever the activity or event, the intent is to create a welcoming experience that helps invited guests discover the warmth of the community, and through this community, it is hoped, the gift of a meaningful relationship to Jesus as Lord. Often great care is taken to make the experience non-threatening, relevant to the

The worship service is seen as the primary place of welcome and invitation.

needs of the guests, interesting, and inspiring. In the congregations most effective with this kind of invitation and welcome, leaders even find intentional ways to motivate and encourage members prior to the activity or event. Tools for invitation, such as cards and brochures, are often provided and the experience is definitely bathed in prayer.

The worship service is seen as the primary place of welcome and invitation. During worship, members regularly are encouraged through sermons, verbal coaching, announcements, and education to bring others to worship with them. Some of the congregations studied also schedule intentional welcome or Friendship Sundays. These Sundays involve concerted efforts encouraging members to invite others to the gathering, planning special activities for the day of the gathering, and intentionally following up with worship visitors after the gathering.

Battle Lake, Minnesota, is a resort community close to the center of the state. Zion makes the most of this by reaching out to seasonal visitors in creative and intentional ways: "We send out a flyer each year in June to 'Boxholder' and offer a 'coupon' for a free cup of coffee . . . which has attracted some attention. We put brochures in area resorts, grocery stores, and campgrounds. We advertise with a picture in area resort periodicals. We have also discovered that word of mouth works well here as well."

Bethlehem Lutheran Church in Sturbridge, Massachusetts, describes itself as a "young, growing congregation eager to welcome you on your first visit! The people want to make you feel at home without being obnoxious. People are eager to learn about God, self, and others here. Some come from a religious background, while others are brand new to the Christian faith. If you're looking for a place to make new friends, be inspired by lively music, and a relevant spiritual message for your daily life; or feel something is missing in your life, try Bethlehem. It's not your ordinary church. You may be surprised at the difference a church can make in your life."

Turning up the temperature on hospitality

A significant factor in effective rural congregations is the attention and focus on hospitality. Having a hospitable, welcoming environment is high on the ministry priority list. The goal is for guests to feel as if they have been welcomed "home." One lay person described her congregation's focus on hospitality by saying, "We swarm them like bees." Effective rural congregations attend to hospitality in ways common to most congregations, with greeters, directions throughout worship, nursery care, a welcome to visitors during the worship service, coffee time following worship, and so on.

Because of their size and their community-centered context, however, rural congregations are able to use some creative, almost homey, ways of signaling hospitality. For example, members of a congregation in South Dakota gather for breakfast each week before worship. One congregation finds ways to regularly decorate the worship space with produce and farm products to lift up its connection to the community. Another congregation offers a unique small group, the Lutheran Brewers Guild, in which participants build community as they sample their home-brewed beer. Other congregations regularly offer baked bread or fresh-off-the-farm pies and pastries as part of their fellowship time.

One rural congregation member described how hospitality was taught in his congregation: "We give people permission to smile and talk. It's OK to chat and visit, and not only is it OK, but it is very important to have that little visiting time as you enter worship. We put the greeters out there. We get the ushers out there. We encourage people to take the risk of introducing themselves to someone even though they may have been worshiping there for 20 years. And even after permission, we have found that some people need to have a little example of how to be friendly. So we teach them. We have a couple of naturally born, gifted people to do that. So the friendliness becomes infectious. It trickles out from the church into the workplace, school, and other places. . . . This has been very important for getting a reputation of being friendly. We have a church sign at the entry to the parking lot that says, 'Zion Lutheran— a friendly people.'" That sign is an external marker for the internal climate regularly nurtured by leaders of this congregation.

Effective rural congregations know their community and reach out in ways that are specific to their context.

In many ways, we keep on pushing congregational awareness of inviting people to church when natural opportunities to do so arise," writes a pastor of Trinity Lutheran Church in Spooner, Wisconsin. "We keep pushing the importance of showing hospitality to our guests. Some examples of how Trinity does this: we serve coffee after services; we send visitors home with a loaf of bread and a note in the package quoting Jesus, 'I am the bread of life' (John 6:35) and expressing the hope that the guest has been well-fed and will return to eat again; we practice open Communion and at the beginning of the service make sure to invite guests to commune. With 65-70% of our county functionally unchurched, we constantly seek to communicate more effectively the good news of what God has done in the world through Jesus Christ. We work to help our members grow in their ministries and have developed ways of reaching into the community. Communicating through evangelism involves active use of brochures, newspaper ads, and a Web site."

Outreach relevant to the context

Effective rural congregations know their community and reach out in ways that are specific to their context. They are in touch with the pulse and needs of their neighbors as well as the calendar and culture of their community. Their evangelism strategies take these realities into account. In the rural farming context of East Lake Andes congregation, South Dakota, effective outreach means attending to the stress and hardship of farm life with support groups for area farmers and an annual Rogation Day service focused on blessing the crops and the workers of the surrounding area. In the changing rural farming and logging community of Everson, Washington, effective outreach means attending to the changing multicultural demographics of the community through English-as-second-language classes and a worship service conducted in Spanish. At Bethel Lutheran Church in Winchester, Virginia, outreach happens by communicating to others in language that highlights "land, stewardship of creation, and covenant."

These congregations do not employ a cookie-cutter approach to evangelism that borrows pre-packaged programs from other places. Instead, they use the natural entrance points made available to them in their context. They are strategic and intentional about making the most of these entry points in ways that truly reach their neighbors.

Tied to the Great Commandment

Vital and effective rural congregations do not intentionally distinguish between evangelism and social ministry. In these places, evangelism is social ministry and social ministry is understood to be evangelism. When pushed, pastors and lay leaders speak to the nuances of evangelism and social ministry. But almost all perceive their caring ministries and social outreach into the community as evangelism and report that their congregations experience growth as a result. Living out the Great Commandment, "loving their neighbors with all their heart, soul, and mind," is a key way members in effective rural congregations bring Jesus' love and presence into their community. Their acts of service and caring convey a sense that the congregation exists for others, knows the basic needs and hopes of its neighbors, and welcomes all kinds of people. Caring ministries in these congregations include: providing food relief to clothing drives; volunteering in local nursing homes and schools;

In these places, evangelism is social ministry and social ministry is understood to be evangelism.

One Wisconsin congregation analyzed its worship attendance and membership growth and noted that a healthy percentage of growth was directly related to work within the community on domestic violence. Leaders from the congregation were instrumental in helping start and staff a county shelter. Congregation members regularly collect supplies for survivors of domestic violence and often assist with finding housing or moving. The congregation opens its doors to host support groups for survivors and batterers at different times. Over time, this significant ministry has helped to build the reputation that this congregation is the place to be.

building houses through Habitat for Humanity; and hosting support groups.

Some non-traditional caring ministries in these places include: farming a dedicated piece of land together and distributing the crops for local needs; offering grief support groups at the hospital and with the local hospice; and hosting a "trash and treasure sale," a rummage sale that facilitates the easy exchange of clothing and goods in a community of deep need.

Growing rural congregations pay attention to children, youth, parents, and families.

In Buffalo, Wyoming, neighbors learn about St. Luke's Lutheran Church through the Christmas Kids' Shoppe. On two Saturdays in December, this ministry makes it possible for children in economically needy families to "shop" for free gifts for up to five family members. Adult family members are treated to refreshments and conversation upstairs while the children shop in the basement. Three hundred children were served the first year, and almost 500 were served the second year. Now the whole community gets involved, with gifts coming from merchants and garage sales. The message of this ministry is clear:

The people of St. Luke's Lutheran Church in Buffalo, Wyoming, readily identify their most successful evangelism effort: a children's choir called the Angels Group. This group, intentionally open to the community, pairs older children with younger ones and teaches singing and clowning. The choir performs in the community and once a month leads worship, which encourages parents and choir members alike to experience worship in the congregation. Also, 40% of those who participate in the Angels Group are not members of the congregation.

At Trinity Lutheran Church in Blanco, Texas, the congregation addresses the needs of the community through a high profile youth ministry. The youth share in worship leadership, Sunday school, community service projects, 5th Quarter Servant Events (free food and drinks for youth following local football games), retreats, lock-ins, camps, and servant trips. This effective ministry has resulted in a reputation as a youth-friendly place, strong appeal to people in the community, and membership growth.

"Through the free gifts, we share our core theology of God's love offered as a gift not earned, but freely given as grace."

Tied to children and family needs

Growing rural congregations pay attention to children, youth, parents, and families. They take seriously Jesus' invitation to let children come, and they find ways to extend into their community by caring for the younger ones. In some contexts, the community infrastructure leaves little for young people to do. In other places, volunteers are needed to support local school activities or community events. Effective rural congregations become engaging and accepting places where young people find fellowship, recreational activities, and service opportunities. These congregations also recognize the needs of parents and look for ways to assist them in nurturing the faith of their children. In addition, members and leaders of these congregations are attentive to the realities of single parent families and blended families and work to promote a healthy sense of welcome in the midst of diversity.

Friends bring friends to Jesus.

Evangelism tied to events and activities

Effective rural congregations operate with the understanding that friends bring friends to Jesus. These congregations therefore provide regular opportunities for members to invite their friends to experience the gathered faith community by intentionally scheduling "friendship" or "welcome" Sundays; fellowship activities, such as a dinner theater or corn roast; youth and family activities; sports events or teams; and community classes. The congregations become hubs for community gatherings through activities that bring meaning and perspective into people's lives.

"They let anyone go there!"

Although these words were first shared as a put-down, over time they have become the slogan for Christ the King Lutheran Church in Durango, Colorado. Effective rural congregations develop a strong and healthy reputation in their community. They are known as caring, welcoming places. In some cases, they are known for specific ministries or services. Their attraction is magnetic, spreading from person to person. In the process of meeting people's relational and physical needs, these congregations offer Jesus. The invited guests become disciples who in turn invite others to come and see.

Best practices for vital ministry

Effective and vital rural congregations demonstrate the following best practices for evangelism:

1. *Friends bring friends.* These congregations practice a friendship evangelism that equips members to invite their friends and neighbors to experience the community and, through the community, Jesus. The

---

Grace Lutheran Church in Mountain Home, Idaho, has developed a reputation in the community with its Spaghetti Dinner Theater. For the past four years, Grace has presented a musical for members of the community to welcome them into the church building and invite them to become active in the congregation.

Planning for the musical begins months in advance with a homegrown script. Then members of the congregation, from young to old, take part in set design, rehearsals, music, dinner preparation, and everything else that goes into staging a play. Although tickets are required, there is no cost for the dinner or the performance. In fact, members are encouraged to give tickets to their friends and neighbors.

Free-will donations are accepted for one of Grace's mission projects. The musical is lighthearted and involves the pastor and key lay leaders.

The message is that the church is a welcoming and fun place. Perhaps the strongest testimony to the evangelistic attraction of this event is that teenagers in town get tickets and come. The church has had to increase the number of performances and the "house" is always full.

During the performances, playgoers receive brochures with information on how to become part of the congregation and join in discipleship. This festive, non-threatening way to invite friends and neighbors has resulted in significant growth in the congregation.

worship service and Jesus are the primary points of invitation, but these congregations also find creative ways to host events or activities that help bring people in contact with the congregation as a faith community.

2. *Energy is devoted to hospitality and welcoming ministries.* These congregations train people to invite and welcome others. Often there are multiple invitations and ways to join congregational activities. Members and leaders are alert to the need to help visitors understand the worship service and to keep the service simple, vital, and energetic. They are good at incorporating new members into the congregation. They develop a strong sense of community through small groups that also provide alternative entry points into the congregation.

3. *Children and youth are priorities.* These congregations are focused on children's outreach and ministries to young people. The congregations feel enthusiastic about the number of youth who are involved and are proud that youth invite friends to come to church with them.

4. *Community involvement is evangelism.* Through social ministries, schools, and community services, these congregations gain high impact and visibility. Many of the congregations are known for a particular social ministry, children's ministry or special program. They see themselves as moving from "maintenance to mission." Their mission orientation causes them to reach out and attend to the needs of their neighbors and community.

Taking it home

Use the following material on your own or as part of a congregation planning group to maximize your understanding of this practice and to discover what you are already doing well and what you might consider strengthening or initiating as a result of your learning.

Individual or group Bible study

When asked which Bible verses best capture their sense of mission, leaders of effective rural congregation leaders chose Matthew 28:18-20 most often. The Great Commission, Jesus' last words to his disciples after the resurrection and just before the ascension, has been the motivation for evangelism and disciple formation since the earliest days of the

church. Read and consider (if you are alone) or discuss (if you are part of a group) Matthew 28:18-20. You may wish to supplement your study by reading other commission texts from the New Testament: Mark 16:15; Luke 24:45-48; John 20:21; and Acts 1:8. Consider the following questions:

1. Imagine you are one of the disciples of Jesus, hearing the Great Commission given to you in your present setting. What would that mean to you and your congregation?

2. How are you already accomplishing the mandate to "go" and to "make disciples"?

3. Describe what you think Jesus might say to you and your congregation today about the practice of evangelism in your setting.

4. Evangelism involves the sharing the good news. Discuss or reflect on the following passages: Luke 4:43; Acts 5:42, Acts 16:10; and 2 Corinthians 4:5.

5. Why did Jesus and his disciples feel such urgency to share God's good news?

6. What is the level of urgency and conviction for evangelism in your congregation? How might you increase the level of hospitality?

7. Discuss or reflect on Matthew 4:23. This passage links the sharing of the gospel with acts of social and public ministry. How is your congregation's social ministry also a form of evangelism? How does this expand your understanding of evangelism?

Celebrating present strengths and ministry

Make a list of your present evangelism ministries and activities. How effective are these efforts in reaching others? If possible, identify two or three initiatives that have been significant in helping your congregation to grow. Celebrate these. If you are unable to name successful initiatives, look at the sampling of evangelism activities at the end of this chapter. Does that list trigger any ideas for hospitality and invitation activities in your congregation?

Extending invitations

Jesus calls us to invite and disciple as he invited and discipled the Twelve. Think of your congregation and community and answer the following questions:

1. What unique opportunities do we have in this place to announce the joy of being a follower of Jesus?

2. Could your congregation be more visible through events and activities in your community?

3. What friends, relatives, newcomers, and visitors living in your community might be waiting for an invitation to come to your church?

Evangelism activities in vital rural congregations

Review the following list of activities. What are you already doing? What might you consider doing or adapting in your setting? Consider discussing these activities with a group.

• Regularly teach members about invitation and friendship evangelism; build a climate that expects members to invite others to worship and other events.

• Follow up with guests through letters, phone calls, and visits by congregation members, as well as the pastor.

• Invite new members through newsletters, local newspaper and radio ads, signs, or billboards in the community.

• Build a reputation in the community through a congregational presence at parades, festivals, and community events.

• Distribute brochures, balloons, or other types of invitations at community events.

• Welcome new residents to the community with intentional visits.

• Know your neighbors and their needs.

• Host special events open to the public, such as a rummage sale, a community dance, or a spaghetti dinner theater, where invitations and information about the congregation are shared.

• Offer choices in worship and music styles, either separate or blended, but always worship with energy and vitality.

• Host "friendship" or "welcome" Sundays periodically.

• Host Christmas or Easter pageants open to the community.

• Provide vacation Bible school, summer camps, and children's ministries in ways that target the needs of the community.

• Design youth activities to welcome community youth; teach youth to invite their friends.

• Provide day care, preschool, or private school connections.

- Offer parenting classes, seminars or groups to members of the community.
- Open the church building to outside groups, such as farmer's support groups, 4-H, Boy Scouts and Girl Scouts, and Alcoholics Anonymous.
- Distribute food, clothing, and other basic necessities to those in need.
- Support a local shelter, nursing home, or social service organization.
- Host servant events and activities open to the community, such as blood drives, hunger walks, Habitat for Humanity projects, and tutoring programs.
- Sponsor or participate in sports teams and opportunities for congregation members or in the neighborhood.
- Provide volunteer and resource support to local schools.

Two action steps

Based on your reading, reflection, and conversation, name two activities you might consider implementing over the next six months to a year. Keep these manageable and achievable. Select ideas that will maximize your evangelism impact in the community and strengthen the invitation skills of your members.

CHAPTER 6

Caring Ministries:
Serving as Jesus Served

Practice: Effective rural congregations make Christ known and develop positive, attractive reputations by stepping out into their neighborhood and world through acts of caring service and social ministry. This social outreach is a natural expression of their discipleship and an ingredient within the mix that contributes to vitality and spiritual energy.

> *"The church exists for the sake of the people who aren't here. Our call is to grow and go. We are saved by grace, through faith, in order to serve. We commit ourselves to: living worship, growing faith, serving fellowship, and sending saints."*

This mission statement from Christ Lutheran Church in Whitefish, Montana, demonstrates the way most growing rural congregations define their purpose: they are there to serve others. This outward focus, an expected outcome of their own faith experience, introduces Jesus and the congregation to the world outside the church doors.

"They Will Know We Are Christians by Our Love" is a popular hymn in many rural congregations. Part of its appeal comes from encouraging acts of kindness and care for others. Jesus tells his followers to love their neighbors as much as they love themselves. Combined with the command to love God with one's whole being, this is said to be the best summary of the Christian life. Vital and effective congregations exhibit a healthy love for their neighbors. Often this is so integral to their Christian lives that it almost goes unnoticed by those who are part of the congregation. It is simply understood to be what "we do together, here in this place, for the sake of others." Patterning themselves after Jesus and his acts of compassion for the disenfranchised, needy, and spiritually hungry people of his day, members of these congregations work to act out their faith and make a difference in their world.

Part of their evangelism appeal

Growing congregations do not engage ministries of service primarily as an evangelism strategy. Their motivation is to love others as Christ has loved them. Nevertheless, the outcome is often evangelistic. People outside the congregation come to know it as a caring community and often find themselves drawn into this community and a relationship with Christ. It's important to be clear about this.

If congregations carry out their ministries in search of money and members, they are soon perceived as shallow and insincere. As a result, their actions seldom translate into numerical growth. On the other hand, those congregations that are genuinely caring tend to exude a charisma that draws others into faith and community.

At Redeemer Lutheran Church in Plymouth, Wisconsin, a dairy town boasting five major cheese processors, the congregation has gained a reputation for service in the community. Activities that have built this reputation include hosting a non-alcoholic New Year's Eve party at the high school for more than 600 teenagers in the community. A local police officer recently drawn to membership in the congregation shared these comments: "If there is something good going on in town, Redeemer is involved in it."

At Christ the King Lutheran Church in Durango, Colorado, what draws others is the effective preschool, work with Habitat for Humanity, and an ongoing soup kitchen ministry. In Mountain Home, Idaho, a former stagecoach stop on the Oregon Trail, Grace Lutheran Church's reputation has been strengthened through counseling services that are offered two days a week. What attracts others to Trinity Lutheran Church in Spooner, Wisconsin, is the congregation's work with children and Helping Hands projects, which get members into the community painting houses, providing food relief, and supporting people with cancer. A lay leader asked to comment about Trinity's appeal replied simply, "What people say about Trinity is that they really know how to take care of people." In effective rural congregations, it is often difficult to know exactly where social ministry stops and evangelism begins.

The congregations themselves don't readily distinguish between social ministry and evangelism. But during further discussion, lay leaders and pastors involved in the research study made the motivation for service very clear and acknowledged that when their congregations serve as Jesus served this brings others to caring community and faith in Christ.

From local to global

There is a tendency for effective rural congregations to focus their caring ministry efforts locally, and then move from the more local context to the wider world beyond them. It is difficult to say which is the stronger priority: reaching out to neighbors near at hand, such as delivering meals-on-wheels, offering grief support, or providing child-care services; or reaching out to neighbors half a world away, for example, by contributing funds to the Heifer Project to send a water buffalo to a village in India. Vital rural congregations view both local and global efforts as important. In a sense, local efforts fuel a more global perspective. Rural congregations often prefer to begin locally. They value the relationships in their community, recognize and respond to the needs of their neighbors, and value seeing their local efforts paying off in concrete ways. Efforts to help those suffering from catastrophic illnesses or accidents can be very successful in these congregations.

Vital rural congregations view both local and global efforts as important.

Consider what happened in rural Lamont, Iowa. Other than the local bar, there was no longer any central meeting place in town where people could get together with one another for support or a good conversation. So the United Methodist church banded together with people from other churches and organizations to create "Common Grounds," a café to serve as the community's meeting place, the headquarters of the local food pantry, the location for an ecumenical Sunday school class for high-school students, and a symbol of Christian unity to the rest of the community.

At Bethel Lutheran Church, a 180-year-old congregation in Winchester, Virginia, the Apple Tree day-care center attracts members of the community. This ministry serves more than 45 children, many of these from outside the church. Another ministry that draws people to Bethel is the annual "Hoe Down Picnic and Dance," an effort that reaches up to seventy-five mentally challenged adults. The congregation addresses local needs like these regularly, but knows that this social ministry focus is even larger. For example, they have a heart for Africa and provide extensive mission support to churches in Tanzania and recently raised funds to build a chaplain's home for the MaaSae Girls Lutheran Secondary School.

Whether at home or beyond, giving and serving others is an important part of the identities and ministry focus of effective rural congregations.

Relevant to the needs of the community

Effective congregations are in touch with their context and know the needs of their neighbors. Members and leaders of these congregations listen well, and seek to position their caring ministries to address the specific needs, hopes, and problems of people and families in the area. Often these needs present themselves simply because of the close relational webs that can exist within smaller rural contexts.

At other times, needs are uncovered and addressed as a result of a formal survey or listening process. In Fordville, North Dakota, where the grain elevator still serves as the focal symbol, leaders of Fordville

Whitefish, Montana, began as a lumber camp and became a major rail yard before it was transformed into a rural resort community near Big Mountain Ski Resort and Glacier National Park.

The prevailing need in this community is health care, and the people of Christ Lutheran have risen to this challenge. The congregation is well-known for the "Shepherd's Hand Clinic," which provides free medical care every Monday night to people who do not qualify for Medicare or Medicaid or have no health insurance.

Congregational leaders point to the clinic as a factor in this faith community's transition from maintenance to mission over the last ten years. (See the congregation's mission statement on page 75, at the beginning of this chapter.)

Lutheran Church worked with their regional judicatory to do a formal needs assessment in the community. In response, the congregation has given more than $40,000 in four years to address concerns identified in the needs assessment.

Although East Lake Andes Lutheran Church may sound like it is close to a resort, it is actually located in the middle of a cornfield in an agricultural community. The context drives the social ministry of this South Dakota congregation. The congregation farms 80 acres of land, with all members buying seed and fertilizer and farmers in the faith community donating their time and equipment. At harvest time, proceeds from the crop are used to fund the church's mission. Through this project and other activities such as an annual Rogation Day service and monthly support group meetings for area farmers, this congregation has gained a reputation for being in touch with its neighbors' lives and needs.

Recently, the congregation at East Lake Andes conducted a formal survey and discovered a need for day care in the area. It is now working to address that need through special grant applications with government agencies. Other practices of this congregation demonstrate the warmth in this caring community: members eat breakfast together at the church every Sunday, youth participate regularly in leading worship, and members are quite active in reaching out to residents in the two nursing care facilities in the area. One lay person writes, "The warm, comfortable feeling this church projects allows a person to be uninhibited and open about their spiritual needs."

Some of the congregations in the research study were indeed small in size but mighty in service.

Move beyond limited thinking

A feeling of smallness can be an obstacle to effective ministry in rural settings. Sometimes this translates into low self-esteem, expressed in comments such as: "We are too few and too small to make a difference. What could our little church do for others? We can barely take care of ourselves." Vital and effective rural congregations move beyond this kind of limited thinking. Some of the congregations in the research study were indeed small in size but mighty in service.

For example, Zion Hill, Pennsylvania, is a small community of no more than 60 homes with an economy driven by small-town retail and manufacturing concerns. Note the extent to which Zion Lutheran Church has gone public with its ministry: "We do Helping Hand projects in which we go out into the community to perform a variety of jobs for the elderly and those in need (painting homes, fixing cars, pouring cement sidewalks, cleaning rain gutters). We provide a food pantry. We collect funds, food, blankets, and clothing for people in need (Kosovo relief, Midwest flood victims, local fire and cancer victims). We offer support groups and outreach to our local nursing and children's homes. We also encourage local groups and organizations to meet regularly in our fellowship hall in order to foster the notion that we are a serving church. These groups include: Girl Scouts, Brownies, Cub Scouts, Boy Scouts, Alcoholics Anonymous, and more. Each year we also host picnics, vacation Bible school, an Easter egg hunt, a Halloween party, blood drives, and several dinners primarily for the sake of our community."

Size and context don't keep these rural congregations from finding creative ways to reach out.

All of the congregations in the research study are involved in ministries of social outreach. While the degree of activity varies from place to place, almost all are involved in basic relief ministries: collecting and distributing food, clothing, quilts, and other resources to people near at hand and far away. Other more involved ministries include ecumenical work with house construction through Habitat for Humanity; children's ministries in the form of preschools, day care, after-school programs, and summer day camp; support groups in the congregation and within local care facilities; and policies that make the church building available to other groups in the community. Size and context don't keep these rural congregations from finding creative ways to reach out.

At Emmanuel Lutheran Church in Everson, Washington, creative outreach happens by providing an English-as-second-language program for

---

In the two-point rural parish of Maynard and Wang in Maynard, Minnesota, 13 members were trained and commissioned to provide pastoral care to the community. Their priorities include visiting elderly people living alone, visiting people with chronic illnesses, and visiting youth.

Spanish-speaking neighbors, welcoming these neighbors in worship with bilingual services, and growing produce in a church garden for distribution at the local food bank.

Leaders at Zion Lutheran Church in Cobleskill, New York, are upfront about the use of their building: "We have vacation Bible school, community musical concerts, and Boy Scouts all using the church. Other groups use the downstairs for community meetings. They are coming into the church for strictly non-church related things, but all around them is information about the church if they are interested."

What goes around comes around

As members of these congregations serve the needs of others, they receive much more in return. Indeed, leaders from effective congregations indicate that caring ministries are key factors in creating vitality and energy within the faith community. People feel the energy. They are blessed by it. And others are drawn into service because of it. Through caring ministries, Christ is made known not only to those served by congregations but also to the congregation themselves.

People feel the energy. They are blessed by it. And others are drawn into service because of it.

Best practices for vital ministry

Effective and vital rural congregations demonstrate the following best practices for caring ministries:

1. Ministries of care and justice are key ingredients to their vitality and attraction. Serving others as Jesus served puts flesh on faith, energizes the faith life and commitment of participating members, and helps build an attractive reputation for the congregation in the community it serves.

2. Ministries of care and justice are relevant to the needs and issues of the community where the congregation exists. Effective congregations know their neighbors, are in tune with their needs, and mobilize members to serve in Christ's name.

3. Evangelism is often a by-product of meaningful caring ministries. The motive for serving is driven by the call to love others as Christ has loved them. Nevertheless, through their serving, lives are touched, drawing people to the congregation that helped them.

4. Serving needs locally leads to a wider sense of mission beyond the community. Growing congregations tend to mobilize around local issues, which often leads people to address concerns beyond the borders of the community.

Taking it home

Use the following material on your own or as part of a congregation planning group to maximize your understanding of this practice and to discover what you are already doing well and what you might consider strengthening or initiating as a result of your learning.

Individual or group Bible study

Read Matthew 25:31-46, Jesus' parable concerning the sheep and goats, and Luke 10:25-37, the parable of the good Samaritan. Both parables reveal Jesus' heart for others and say something about the mandate he has given his followers. As you reflect on the meaning in these passages, consider the following questions:

1. Why do you think Jesus makes the matter of feeding the hungry, giving drink to the thirsty, clothing the unclothed, and visiting those in prison so important?

2. What does it mean to you and your congregation to know that you serve Jesus when you serve others?

3. What does it mean to you when Jesus connects the matter of eternal life to being a neighbor to others?

4. What might being a good Samaritan entail in your community?

Celebrating present strengths and ministry

The stories and examples in this chapter may spark ideas for unique opportunities that call for mission in your community. Follow these simple steps to capture your ideas about future possibilities:

1. List your present service ministries. Which ones are you most proud of? Which reflect Christ's heart and make Christ known in your community? Are there any that should receive less focus or attention?

2. Individually or as a group, take time to reflect on your community context. What are the needs in your community? You may consider

taking a survey. Check in with the local government office, school, or law enforcement agency for information. List concerns and needs, then prioritize these based on your congregation's interests, gifts, and resources. Add any ideas that you found helpful as you read this chapter.

Two action steps

Based on your reading, reflection and conversation, name two activities you might consider implementing over the next six months to a year. Keep them manageable and achievable. Select the ideas that will maximize your congregation's caring ministries.

CHAPTER 7

Leadership:
Who's Driving the Tractor?

Practice: Effective rural congregations model a shared leadership in which the pastor's role is significant, yet not dominant; the role of laity is active rather than passive; and Jesus is seen as the primary leader for all in the congregation to follow.

"The history of our church traditionally involved the pastor serving as the proprietor of the shop. If something needed doing, the pastor would see to it. With this approach, the church was limited to the abilities of the pastor. It became a small, frugal, family church. Serving the needs of the existing congregation became central to the church and the vision was lost. With this self-centered attitude and a change in the local economy and demographics, the church quickly found itself in a survival mode. Most of the issues discussed around the church involved money and paying the bills. With the decision to embrace a new future, we found that the old wounds could finally be healed over with tender new skin. A new start was made and our future was filled with a fresh vision from Jesus."

This quote powerfully summarizes the leadership shift going on in effective rural congregations. For the most part, these congregations are leaving behind older models that position the pastor or a few pillar families as the ones "driving the tractor." Instead, these congregations are experimenting with new patterns of shared leadership drawn from the model of Jesus as servant-leader and uniting pastor and laity around a common vision for their future.

Indeed, this practice of shared leadership appears to be a necessary ingredient to congregational vitality and renewal. As people are empowered to work together and embrace their baptismal, God-given calls, an energy is released that allows the congregation to accomplish significant ministry for members and others. Shared leadership ultimately means more people are engaged. The team spirit that emerges from shared leadership helps lay members view ministry as the work of the people—a joyous privilege instead of a duty, an opportunity instead of a task.

Leadership is about following

"Good leaders are followers who are also leaders," quipped one lay member of a focus group. Leadership is like a dance in which someone can take the lead sometimes and follow at other times. Members of the congregation perceive the pastor to be an important leader in the congregation but also a follower, someone who follows Jesus as the primary leader and also willingly follows lay leaders who step into specific roles or ministries.

In this model of shared leadership, people pass the baton of leadership back and forth to each other.

Lay leaders in these congregations not only respect and honor their pastors, they also mobilize and guide other members. Those who are mentored by lay leaders and the pastor continue to carry leadership forward. In this model of shared leadership, people pass the baton of leadership back and forth to each other. This model builds on a foundation of respect, honoring people as gifted and using a Romans 12 perspective that all parts of the body are necessary and can take the lead when needed.

Another way to describe this leadership tango might be to suggest that leadership in these congregations is flexible rather than rigid. These congregations do not have top-down leadership in which a commander issues orders and subordinates follows. Instead, there is a sense that God is the master leader and individuals can step in and out of leadership roles.

Leadership is following Jesus

Ultimately, Jesus is the leader everyone in the congregation seeks to follow. Through prayer, Bible study, and conversation, pastors and lay leaders in vital congregations seek to discern Jesus' will for their work together. They pattern their activities and their leadership style on Jesus:

"Jesus knew that the Father had put all things under his power, and that he had come from God and was returning to God; so he got up from the meal, took off his outer clothing, and wrapped a towel around his waist. After

that, he poured water into a basin and began to wash his disciples' feet, drying them with the towel that was wrapped around him" (John 13:3-5, New International Version).

These congregations embrace images of Jesus as servant leader. Jesus loved others in life-transforming ways. trained others by employing a multitude of creative teaching strategies. Jesus was gentle but decisive; he loved others but also challenged them. Jesus called people to walk the narrower way and supported them on that journey. He built hope and community as lives were touched and changed.

"Leaders step up, but don't care about having power. They are humble, but don't need the credit. They have a servant's heart, are collaborative, wise, have no time for mediocrity, they are not about maintaining the status quo."

"A leader is a person of integrity, one who is trustworthy, one who can take a congregation from one step to the next, who acts as a beacon to help others see in which direction to go."

"Leaders have an authentic relationship with God."

The pastor as leader is critical

These congregations embrace images of Jesus as servant leader.

Pastors play a significant role in vital, growing congregations. All of the congregations in the final phase of the research study had pastors who were regarded as spiritual leaders, motivational teachers and preachers, and caring, encouraging friends. These pastors lead in non-coercive, gift-affirming ways. They walk their talk, are transparent and available to their people, and regularly invite others into the adventure of faith and discipleship. They coach, empower, and even cajole people to own their calls to ministry and leadership. These pastors aren't necessarily the most eloquent or most charismatic leaders, yet they are known to be warm, genuine, and faithful. These pastors have earned the respect of their people through caring, servant-like ministry. Through them, Christ is made known and becomes real for congregations.

While clearly modeling mutual partnership in ministry, these pastors also know they are called to lead. "The pastor should never forget that she or he is the spiritual director in the rural congregation," shared a pastor from Montana.

"Whatever else he or she may be, the pastor should never relinquish that role. Nothing can take the place of that. It is what we are called to do." Pastors of vital congregations identify their primary role as symbolizing and articulating the spirituality and vision of the congregation. How this is carried out has great influence on the rest of the congregation. If this is done well, other leaders develop to articulate and expand the spiritual vision and focus of the congregation. If pastors are jealous or protective of their authority or leadership positions, others are prevented from growing in authority or expanding their roles. When pastors lead others to a fuller appreciation of their gifts and empower them to take on spiritual and programmatic leadership, either within or outside of the faith community, the whole congregation grows together.

When asked what is important in a pastor, one lay leader replied, "Love the people, love the people, love the people. If that's not there, no amount of leadership will do." The leadership model of the pastor as a friend and one who loves the congregation is essential in rural settings. There is a deep and abiding sense that the pastor is one who genuinely cares, is willing to walk alongside people and even go the extra mile. Members perceive their pastor as a caring presence, as someone guiding, affirming, working alongside them, and willing to get his or her hands dirty doing the most basic work of the congregation. Pastors gain respect in these places by practicing a ministry of presence and visitation with their people.

The fit between the pastor and congregation is critical. Pastors in vital rural congregations genuinely like their congregations and settings and have served or plan to serve in the same place for quite some time. When pastors don't like their congregations or the rural context, the vitality of

There is a deep and abiding sense that the pastor is one who genuinely cares, is willing to walk alongside people and even go the extra mile.

In Fordville, North Dakota, "the congregation's reputation hangs on the pastor," writes one lay leader. "He is the only resident pastor in our community and he sometimes feels he has his main ministry at the café with 9:00 a.m. coffee. His presence is very much appreciated by members of the community."

the faith community is affected. When a pastor's commitment is seen as authentic, members of a congregation get excited and engaged in ministry. Effective pastors are committed to the long haul, and work patiently and tenderly to gain the support and partnership of the people they serve. During the research study, several pastors highlighted the value of longevity, sharing that it took up to three years of servant leadership to gain the full trust of members in their congregations.

Shared leadership

These leaders consistently and consciously encourage members to remember, serve, and invite their neighbors.

The extent to which leadership is shared in effective congregations became evident to one person recording comments during the focus group phase of the research study: "It wasn't until the leadership questions that I became aware of who the pastors were. Yet one could tell the laity had respect for their pastors by the comments they made. The group was respectful and courteous of one another in sharing their stories. When a new idea or approach came up, you could hear comments from the pastors and the laity alike: 'Maybe we should try that,' and 'What a good idea!'"

Because lay representatives and clergy all shared confidently and proudly about ministry in their settings, they could not easily be distinguished from each other. Their words, actions, and behaviors revealed the extent to which ministry was truly shared.

How does shared ministry happen? One possibility is that pastors in effective rural congregations are not threatened by the abilities of lay leaders. Rather, they are pleased and proud of the leadership and abilities of their lay leaders. These pastors have learned that they do not need to do all the speaking or have all the answers.

Leadership in vital rural congregations is permission-giving. The pastors help people discern their gifts, inspire leadership through preaching and Bible study, and help connect people to meaningful ministries. Although it can be difficult to build a leadership cadre among people who sometimes feel unempowered or uncertain about their skills, these pastors build leadership creatively and work at it consistently. They foster a can-do attitude, and then getting out of the way as soon as possible.

The leadership style at St. Andrew's Lutheran Church in South Glen Falls, New York, a health-care and commuter community, results in shared decision-making: "The leadership style in our congregation is informal, casual, and friendly. It is a very permission-giving type of leadership, very democratic. Because we function as teams (versus committees), there is no one leader. All decisions are made as a team. Council merely approves or disapproves action from the team. The pastor is more in an overview capacity versus the one person who makes all of the decisions. The leaders in the congregation are willing to fail and to take risks. That makes them effective leaders."

Effective leaders cast a vision of mission

Pastors and lay leaders in effective congregations care for the needs of their present members through pastoral care, effective teaching and preaching, and ongoing events and activities that build community and strengthen the bonds of the gathered family. But these pastors don't stop there. Ultimately, they practice for those who are not yet part of the family. Leaders in effective congregations have an uncanny ability to keep the focus of the congregation outward. Through studying, planning, preaching, and teaching, these leaders consistently and consciously encourage members to remember, serve, and invite their neighbors.

This happens in a significant way through the development of mission statements and by engaging in strategic planning processes. These times of planning and reflection take their cues from biblical study and prayer. They are seen as primary ways to discern God's will for the congregation. Growing congregations then look for ways to keep this vision posted and printed often, through communication with the entire congregation and as a regular part of ministry team meetings.

"We were 75 years old in 2000," writes a leader from Christ Lutheran Church in Whitefish, Montana. "For 50 years we were a very traditional Scandinavian church, small and very stable. Isolated. For the last 10 years we have moved from maintenance to mission. From control to ministry. We have put ministry into the hands of the laity. The pastor is a model and an equipper who trains, and then hands off ministry." This

Casting a vision for a mission-focused ministry takes time and needs to honor context.

transition has occurred through a focus on mission, patient teaching, and the development of a simple mission statement that carries as its key words: "Living worship, growing faith, serving fellowship, and sending saints." The congregation operates from a theology of abundance that celebrates the belief that God provides all of the resources, talents, and people needed to accomplish ministry. This expectation for high commitment yields abundant results.

Casting a vision for a mission-focused ministry takes time and needs to honor context. It's important to listen and learn, to discover the heartbeat and needs of the community (both the congregation as community and the surrounding community), to take time to study, pray, and discern together the Spirit's prompting. Although they clearly take the lead in this process, pastors can't superimpose their own visions on a congregation. A vision can't simply be imported from elsewhere. It must be relevant to a particular place. Effective congregations develop a shared vision between clergy and laity that for the most part has all people playing off the same sheet of music together.

Listen in to this conversation between two pastors (**A** and **B**) in the research study:

A: I had a pastor tell me before accepting this call: "Don't even create a vision or mission statement for the first year." . . . What he was getting at was take time to get to know the congregation and the community to see what their dreams and visions are. Then the exciting struggle is piecing all the visions together.

B: I agree. In our experience it's important to take time to get to know who we are and what God is working in us and in the community. If you are moving from one place to another, you don't just import a vision and say it's going to work here.

A. It's been interesting, because now the congregation is at a point [of embracing their ministry]. We have just gone through a six-month process of drawing together stories to create our vision. My sense is that the process has really taken about three years. It began with cottage visits where members met in various homes. God is doing some pretty powerful things through this process.

Effective leaders can initiate change

Change for change's sake can cause conflict. As one pastor shared: "Give them the *why* and then let them be involved in the *how*." For the most part, leaders in growing congregations appear comfortable with taking risks. They are willing to try new things and abandon old practices that don't work so well anymore. Most leaders in growing congregations believe that change is positive because it moves people off of the status quo and provides a new sense of what is possible.

One of the places where change is most evident is in the organizational structure of these congregations. Many of them are shifting from a committee-driven, business-like model to ministry teams that are more streamlined and action-focused. In these teams, attention often goes to Bible study and prayer as well as the work they are called to do. Organizational structure is more fluid and organic. The pastor is not always expected to be present. There is permission to try some things and encouragement to risk failure as well.

Effective leaders manage conflict

Conflict is a given in congregational life, and congregations that are moving to an outward orientation that includes the neighbor will experience turbulence. Leaders in growing congregations know this. They expect it and they address it head-on when it occurs.

Trinity Lutheran Church in Spooner, Wisconsin, is typical of many of the congregations in this study. With the arrival of a clergy couple committed to mission, the congregation began a transformation process that has resulted in several new ministry offerings for the community, among them a contemporary worship service and a regular "kids' church" experience. For these and other reasons, conflict erupted, making for a couple of tough years for the congregation. With patience and perseverance, most of the conflict has been resolved.

"We went from being thousands of dollars behind each month a few years ago to being thousands ahead now. The change is due to fighting and settling well a long overdue power struggle. People have said it was a good fight for Trinity. It weeded out some crabs and got other people awake and more involved," said one member of the congregation.

> We have a small council, made up of gifted, capable leaders who have the authority and a lot of permission, repeated often, to go ahead and get things done. Beyond the council, there are many gifted people who are given permission and freedom to do things and experiment."—*from Trinity in Spooner, Wisconsin*
>
> The gift of the rural community is you can see who your potential leaders are and observe them for their gifts. The downside is a limited pool. But there are creative ways to approach potential leaders in a rural setting. Simply say, 'I see you have these skills, would you . . .' It's important to meet them where they are and grow together. Start with a small task that is not too threatening. Get to know their boundaries and limits. Develop that little bit of confidence and it almost always goes a long way.

The congregation is on the other side of the conflict now and experiencing new energy and growth. When asked how he helped members face the conflict, one of the pastors shared: "I ask, what does the New Testament say? In most of those books, conflict was an issue. There's lots of conflict in the church. It's a given and we simply have to face it and walk through it."

Effective leaders are trained

"There's lots of conflict in the church. It's a given and we simply have to face it and walk through it."

Effective leaders are intentionally recruited and trained utilizing a variety of approaches. In rural congregations the pastor is often the primary recruiter and trainer, and views this role as an important part of his or her ministry. The pastor is constantly discerning who could be invited to a leadership role; training others for leadership through preaching and teaching; and encouraging and mentoring as new leaders step up to the plate.

The role of the pastor as shepherd and cheerleader is strong in growing rural congregations. Pastors walk with new leaders until they are brave enough to walk on their own. In fact, in most of these congregations there seems to be a kind of apprenticeship model with four steps: 1) I do, you watch; 2) We do together; 3) You do, I watch; 4) You do it alone.

Another pastor shared, "Part of being an effective leader is seeing the spark in some of those people who don't come forward themselves and then to motivate them and give them an opportunity."

One key way that growing congregations encourage leadership is through a gifts-discernment-and-deployment process. Through the use of inventories and regular teaching and preaching about spiritual gifts, these congregations help people discover how God has gifted them and how they can best lead based on their gifts. The intent is to avoid slot filling. Instead, by prayer and the guidance of the Holy Spirit, we are not asking volunteers, but instead, asking the right people. (For information on spiritual gifts inventories, see the resource list on pages 114-116.)

Several pastors offered another key to promoting lay leadership: "Be strategic and start small"; "Jesus changed the world with 12 people." In effective rural congregations, the pastor intentionally focuses on a few key lay members for leadership development. This "trainer of trainers" approach maximizes leadership and nurtures those who can effectively lead others.

Leadership training in these congregations takes place in a variety of creative ways. These include: reading books together and watching interactive video workshops that model new ideas and strategies; attending training events sponsored by the judicatory or national body of the church; visiting teaching congregations from similar or different contexts where mission is modeled and ministry is effective.

For several of these congregations, leadership retreats are the most helpful venue for training leaders. These retreats are led either by leaders of the congregation or by outside leaders with experience in mobilizing ministry. In addition, leaders from two congregations in the final phase of the research study spoke about receiving support and encouragement from judicatory staff, particularly when issues of conflict need to be addressed.

These congregations help people discover how God has gifted them and how they can best lead based on their gifts.

Leading with prayer and study

To sum up this chapter, leadership in growing congregations appears to be more about *being* than *doing*. It is more about being a disciple in touch and in tune with Jesus as the master leader than being a worker with a tool kit and a talent for fixing things.

To a great degree, effective rural congregations incorporate Bible study and prayer into the flow of their working teams. At Trinity Lutheran Church in Spooner, Wisconsin, for example, council meetings are roughly divided in thirds: one-third Bible study, one-third visioning and prayer, and one-third business. As people grow and pray together, the church's work takes on energy and renewed meaning.

Best practices for vital ministry

Effective and vital rural congregations demonstrate the following best practices for leadership:

1. Jesus is the model and the ongoing center of congregational life. The congregations pattern leadership on Jesus and seek his insight in prayer, Bible study, worship, preaching, and committees or ministry teams.

2. The pastor's role as leader is critical and essential. As pastors in effective rural congregations mentor and encourage others to a deeper expression of discipleship, they hold several qualities in tension: they are strong and caring, decisive and collaborative, willing to lead and able to follow, the voice of God and a personal friend.

3. Lay members express their faith actively in the ministries of their congregation. They can identify their spiritual gifts and are mentored, trained, and supported in the work they feel called to do inside and outside of the congregation.

4. Leadership training is constant and ongoing. Leadership is viewed to be an expression of discipleship and is nurtured and encouraged through preaching, teaching, study, and ongoing conversation.

Taking it home

Use the following material on your own or as part of a congregation planning group to maximize your understanding of this practice, to discover what you are already doing well and what you might consider strengthening or initiating as a result of your learning.

Individual or group Bible study

Read Philippians 2:1-8 and 1 Thessalonians 2:7b-12. The first passage reflects the church's earliest understanding of Jesus as servant leader. Consider the meaning of this passage in light of the foot washing text highlighted earlier in this chapter. The second passage offers Paul's insights into his work as a leader and teacher among the people of Thessalonica.

1. What do these passages suggest about leadership?

2. Make a list of the leadership values you find in these texts. Which of these values is demonstrated in your congregation?

3. How might you understand the role of the pastor differently in light of these texts?

Celebrating present strengths and ministry

Follow this process to reflect on leadership in your congregation:

1. *Name your present leadership style and structure.* Draw a picture or draft a statement that best reflects the way leadership is done in your congregation. Share insights if you are part of a group. What do you notice? What do you appreciate? What is not so helpful? Do the leaders in your congregation study and pray together?

2. *Review your congregation's current vision and mission statement (if you have one).* Does it reflect the direction and purpose of the congregation? Do people know your reason for being? Is it time to reengage or start a strategic planning process that might lead toward the development of a new mission statement?

3. *List new learning worth more reflection or action.* What insights about leadership in effective rural congregations did you discover in this chapter? What specific ideas or strategies might be worth initiating in your setting? Which ideas could strengthen your present leadership orientation?

Two action steps

Based on your reading, reflection, and conversation, name two activities you might consider implementing over the next six months to a year. Keep them manageable and achievable. Select the ideas that will maximize the practice of shared leadership in your congregation.

CHAPTER 8

Context: Discovering the Gift of Place

"We celebrate and embrace a rural agricultural life where farming is the primary focus for our community."

"Ours is a nice, clean, rural, middle-class, blue-collar town where people are friendly."

"We serve in a community where recreation is the draw and many commute great distances for work and shopping."

"In our community, the grain elevator is the focal symbol. We describe ourselves as being a small, nice, quiet, safe community. Someone is always there to help you, and everyone knows your business."

Like the individual snowflakes that fall on the fields of North Dakota or the one-of-a-kind fingerprints of miners in Pennsylvania, each congregation has a unique context and place. Dozens of factors contribute to the look and feel of a particular congregation in a particular place. The age of the congregation; its history and ethnic background; the gifts of its present members; the community where it is planted; the focus of the community in terms of vocation and economy; the length of pastorates; and whether it's a single-point, two-point, multipoint, or parish ministry are just some of the influences that give a congregation its orientation and character. A key to effective ministry is acknowledging, celebrating, and using the gifts of a congregation's place and its people.

Jujitsu is a martial art form that harnesses and releases great energy and power. Those who practice jujitsu learn to receive and capture the energy coming at them from an opponent. They turn this energy around and make it work for them, not against them. Through this discipline, some people can defend themselves from opponents two or three times their weight. In a sense, effective congregations receive, capture, and release the energy of the gifts of place and people, harnessing a power that contributes to a vital and meaningful ministry.

This power is not released when one congregation's programs are simply transferred to another place. Dynamic and successful ministry must always be contextualized with sensitivity to the history, available resources, and the needs of the congregation and community.

Vital and effective congregations find renewed hope and confidence in discovering, celebrating, and using their gifts in ways suited to their settings. They avoid negative thinking, which makes us lose perspective and prevents us from seeing possibilities and opportunities.

A key to effective ministry is acknowledging, celebrating, and using the gifts of a congregation's place and its people.

Celebrating the gifts of a rural context

Although many of the practices highlighted in this book are not necessarily exclusive to rural settings, there are unique gifts of place that can be celebrated and successfully used in most rural contexts. Like many gifts, these can manifest a downside if they are not used in a positive manner.

High visibility and reputation

The smaller size and population density of rural settings makes it possible for congregations to stand out more forthrightly in the eyes of their neighbors. This can be particularly so for congregations that develop "signature ministries" which address specific needs within the community, such as a preschool, a local sports league, or support for survivors of abuse. In fact, in a number of settings, the congregation's building serves as a focal point for the surrounding community, in some cases even designating the center of town.

A congregation's presence and ministry is often easier to communicate to the community in rural settings. Access to local media is cheaper and more effective. Marketing strategies such as the use of brochures, mailings, displays at community events, newspaper and radio ads, and community posters and billboards have greater impact. The close relational ties in these communities also provide for "friendship evangelism," the form of outreach that encourages friends to invite friends.

The downside of this gift is captured in the old adage: "It takes a lifetime to build a reputation, only a moment to destroy it." Activities that tarnish a rural congregation's reputation can destroy a good reputation that may have taken years to build. It is also the case that a negative reputation can stay with rural congregations longer than congregations in other settings.

The unique place of the pastor

Small system changes are not only possible, but make a difference in these settings.

The pastor's role and power of presence in the community is often stronger in rural settings. Because of the size of the community, the pastor may be one of just a handful of official leaders in the community. Pastors in these settings often are able to practice a ministry of presence and care that has a positive impact far beyond the congregation.

The pastor's role within the faith community is also somewhat different in these settings. Visitation of members in their homes and on their farms is still effective and highly valued, and members often regard their pastor as a friend.

The downside of this gift is seen if a pastor misuses authority and loses the trust of the people. Trust is critical in these settings and grows slowly, layer by layer, over several years. Once trust is built and members perceive their pastor as genuine, they are likely to follow the pastor into just about any challenge or ministry opportunity.

Event evangelism

Event evangelism works in rural and small-town settings. Event evangelism is a strategy in which congregations offer events and activities to the community and encourage members to invite their friends. If these activities are targeted to meet specific relational, emotional, educational, or physical needs of community members, the impact can be great. Events such as concerts, special worship services, dinners, plays, pageants, rummage sales, classes, and support groups attract neighbors for many reasons. These activities often involve friends, and they meet strong relational needs for people in settings that are sometimes isolated and remote.

Openness to the new

In effective rural congregations, there appears to be a greater openness to new ideas, new ministry opportunities, and new people. This perspective is part of the vitality and freshness that can be so attractive in these places.

An organic spirituality

Vital rural congregations experience and express the organic connections between their context and their worship, theology, and spirituality. In rural agricultural settings this is often seen in imagery related to land, growth, seasons, and harvest. The congregation's sense of place shapes its ministry and culture. In these settings, people tend to think more organically than mechanically. In a mechanically oriented culture, something that is broken is fixed by following a pattern of logical steps. In contrast, in an organically oriented culture, solutions are grown, nurtured, and tended. They are looked at as a whole and shaped by the all of the influences that can be brought to bear on the situation.

Intergenerational ties

Pastors and lay leaders often find that an intergenerational ministry focus is effective and easier to implement in rural settings. Although intergenerational ministry might begin out of necessity, by clustering classes and groups of people due to fewer numbers, some wonderful connections can be made across generations.

Support for children and families

The saying "It takes a village to raise a child" rings especially true in rural settings. Children often find several adults they can relate to as role models and mentors. Parents also find a sense of community and support for their parenting needs. In many rural areas, there is great sensitivity to the needs of single parents and families in special situations. It is common for children from the community who have not attended church to be "adopted" by the congregation and nurtured in their faith and relationships.

The impact of individuals

In rural settings, a single voice can be heard and appreciated. Small system changes are not only possible, but make a difference in these settings. Change can be facilitated one-on-one as people work together. The gifts of individuals who step forward in leadership are welcomed and can truly have impact in the congregation and community.

The downside of this gift is that it is also easy for one or two people to dominate and make most of the decisions.

Your congregation's place in community

There is no simple way to define what makes a place *rural*. Part of this is due to changing economics and demographics. At the beginning of the 21st century, the term *rural* is very different from what rural was in the year 1900. So how might a congregation best understand its geographical context? If older labels don't quite fit, are there new ways to identify context that might make it easier to understand and use the gifts of place?

In the book *Land and Community* (Guelph: University of Guelph, 1988) Canadian sociologist R. Alex Sim identifies four primary settings that rural congregations find themselves in today, each with its attendant joys and challenges for ministry. These four types are: Ribbonvilles, Agravilles, Might-have-been-villes, and Fairviews.

Ribbonville

Ribbonvilles are small towns that surround a city, sometimes called "collar counties." Most of these towns were once township trade centers for farmers. As cities have grown and pushed out to suburbs and beyond, developing broader metropolitan areas, many of these once primarily rural places find themselves in transition. Some become "bedroom" or "commuter" communities with residents who travel more than an hour in one direction to get to their jobs. With the advent of at-home technology, telecommuting has made even the more remote rural community an ideal place to call home. Ribbonvilles are communities in transition. The tension of life lived in several worlds comes together in these places.

Congregations in Ribbonville have some special challenges and opportunities. There is potential for growth, but often not without the price of change. Family churches steeped in history and tradition find they must reinvent themselves if they are going to be welcoming to their newer neighbors. For the most part, people in these congregations still call themselves rural, but their self-understanding is affected by the demographic shifts going on in their community.

Agraville

Sim defines Agravilles as farm-service towns, like those where Kmart or Wal-Mart began business. The economic base of the community is often agricultural, although in some cases it is based on other extractive activities such as mining and logging.

Congregations in these settings need to be aware of the culture and economy of their area.

Agravilles may have 2,500 to 50,000 residents, with many more people living within a radius of 30 miles. These communities are often farther from a major metropolitan area the Ribbonvilles and often have a distinct culture and flavor. People come to Agraville to shop and for medical, educational, and governmental services.

There usually are several churches in Agraville, some with a long history in the community. A rural mind-set can still be very much a factor in shaping the life and flavor of congregations in this context, but influences driven by information technology (such as the Internet) have helped to usher in changes for ministry in these settings.

Agravilles are influenced by the primary economic activities in their areas. Congregations in these settings need to be aware of the culture and economy of their area because these will influence people's values, lifestyle, hopes, and struggles. Residents may speak of these communities as being ideal places to live.

Might-have-been-ville

For Sim, Might-have-been-villes are the thousands of villages and small towns that find themselves in the shadow of Agravilles. Residents of Might-have-been-villes often recall better days when the area was lively and things were happening in the community. Instead of counting on the local doctor who used to make house calls, people commute to Agraville to a clinic that is part of a group practice. It is not uncommon for children to be picked up and bussed more than 10 miles to attend school in Agraville.

Might-have-been-ville congregations range from thriving to dying. Those that are vital have found ways to be a beacon of hope and influence in their community. They have leveraged the assets of their ministries to serve themselves and others well. Rural values shape their identity and ministry. Sometimes these congregations are known for signature ministries that serve the community, such as day-care programs or dynamic youth ministry. Those that are struggling and dying find it difficult to generate the salary to pay their pastor. They may not have been willing to embrace some necessary changes in ministry. In some cases, economic and cultural realities beyond their control make it impossible to continue anymore. A number of creative options for ministry can be found in these places: yoked congregations, cooperative parishes, designated lay leadership, and pastors who pursue a second vocation outside of their faith communities.

Fairview

Sim uses the term Fairview to describe rural communities founded on recreational activities, including water sports, fishing, camping, or skiing. Some Fairviews are popular destination points for people vacationing from other places, and they may serve as comfortable retirement communities.

Fairview congregations struggle with seasonal fluctuations in attendance. They experience the tension of being a part of a rural, small-town culture in which there is a constant influx of diversity and new ideas. They can thrive by developing focused ministries that meet the needs of their community.

For a fuller description of these types and their implications for congregational life, see chapter 4 of *Rural Ministry: The Shape of the Renewal to Come* (Abingdon, 1998), by Shannon Jung et al.

To these four settings that Sim describes, we add one more: Countryville.

Countryville

By Countryville we mean to identify and include those congregations that find themselves doing ministry in traditional rural country settings. These are the hundreds of congregations in North America in the open country, surrounded by fields and farms and often located a few miles from the nearest town.

Congregations in these places are truly shaped by agriculture or the single industry economy of their context. Their way of life takes its orientation from the primary vocation of people in the surrounding area.

Congregations in these settings often are multi-point parishes, or congregations served by part-time pastors or lay leaders. When they are vital, these congregations are the glue of their communities, bringing people together for social, educational, and spiritual needs. Effective congregations in this context become a primary source for support, entertainment, growth, and community for people who find themselves in more remote settings with fewer options.

What specific rural gifts can you name and identify in your place?

Taking it home

What is special and important about your congregation and the community in which it exists? Do you find your congregation in one of the five typologies described above? What specific rural gifts can you name and identify in your place?

Use the following questionnaire to gather information about your congregation and your context for ministry. This questionnaire is adapted from the fuller set of questions used by the 26 congregations participating in the final phase of the research study. (Some of the questions utilized in the research study for this book were gleaned and adapted from "Thirty Questions to Answer Concerning A Rural Community," in L. Shannon Jung's book *Rural Congregation Studies: A Guide for Good Shepherds* (Abingdon, 1997, pp. 55-65).

Gather a representative group of leaders in your congregation to answer these questions together. Dedicate two or more hours to this exercise. Capture and summarize your discoveries in writing and use them to shape your conversation and planning for the future.

1. How did the community where your congregation is located come to be? What was the founding goal or dream upon which the community was built?

2. What is you community's focal symbol (for example, a grain elevator or courthouse square)?

3. What are your community's chief economic functions? How do people make a living? What is the routine and rhythm of their work?

4. How would you describe your community to an interested visitor? Describe the people, the environment, the makeup of subgroups, and the perceived needs of the residents.

5. What kind of reputation does your church have in the community? What does the grapevine say about you?

6. What two or three ministries are you most known for in the community?

7. What is the relationship between your church and the other congregations in your community?

8. If your congregation were a living, breathing being, what would it look like? What might be overdeveloped? What might be underdeveloped?

9. What makes your congregation's heart "sing"? What two or three things about your congregation should be celebrated?

10. In a nutshell, how might you describe your congregation's history and culture (age of congregation, background, role of clergy, points of conflict, celebrations, and so fourth)?

11. What might a representative of each of the following age groups point to as the most important ministry you offer or engage in: people under 20; people ages 20-40; people 40-65; people 65 and up?

12. Brainstorm a list of ministry offerings to the community of which you are most proud. What are the top three to five activities that have contributed to your congregation's vitality and growth? Answer the same questions for ministry offerings that are more focused on the membership of the congregation.

13. What are the assets of your present members? Review your congregation's membership list and think about the gifts already present in your congregation. What patterns do you see emerging? What gifts could be used for future ministry?

14. Of the five types for rural settings identified in this chapter, which best describes your community? Ribbonville, Agraville, Might-have-been-ville, Fairview, or Countryview? Does your setting closely fit with one type, is it more of a blend, or does your congregation belong to completely different category?

15. Which of the rural gifts identified in this chapter can you claim and use as part of your identity? Are there other gifts in your setting that weren't identified here?

CHAPTER 9

Mission: Possible— Discovering Hope for the Future

"Do not remember the former things, or consider the things of old. I am about to do a new thing; now it springs forth, do you not perceive it? . . . for I give water in the wilderness, rivers in the desert, to give drink to my chosen people, the people whom I formed for myself so that they might declare my praise" (Isaiah 43:18-21).

On the *Mission: Impossible* TV show of the 1960s and 1970s, the leader of a group of special agents received a message at the beginning of each episode: "Your mission, should you choose to accept it, is to . . ." Each mission was remarkably complicated and almost impossible to complete. But somehow through wit, cunning, and special gadgetry, it always turned out possible after all.

Sometimes ministry feels like *Mission: Impossible,* particularly in rural congregations. Limited size, financial constraints, congregational history, and negative self-image can cause pastors and members to feel hopeless and ineffective. In fact, in a survey of pastors conducted for the book *Turnaround Strategies for the Small Church* (Ron Crandall, Abingdon Press, 1995, p. 42), negative self-image was shown to be the number one problem facing smaller churches by a 2-to-1 margin.

Negative self-image is the silent killer of many churches today. Tired of trying, worn out by limited thinking, and burdened by economic realities, many congregations become complacent, turn in upon themselves, and give up—sometimes without fully realizing they are doing this.

But mission is possible in rural settings! Effective rural congregations in the research study and in all denominations across the nation offer proof of this. The real experts on vitality in rural settings are those congregations and leaders experiencing it firsthand. Their stories reveal hope and their practices can be replicated in other rural settings. May God bless you as you engage in mission in your corner of this world!

Building an action plan for your future

If you have been using this book as a small group resource over a period of several weeks or months, you have discovered that much that can be applied to ministry in your congregation. Use the following worksheet to review the practices of vital rural congregations and to capture your thoughts and intentions for follow-up. Develop an action plan that reflects what you have learned and positions your congregation for a hopeful future.

Mission is possible in rural settings! Effective rural congregations in the research study and in all denominations across the nation offer proof of this.

Six practices for effective ministry

Practice 1: Prayer—Letting go and letting God

Effective rural congregations are spiritually alert, and regular and intentional in their prayer life and activity. They seek Jesus' power, guidance, and direction in their planning and ministry.

1. Key insights concerning this practice include:

_____

_____

_____

2. The two action steps identified are:

a. _____

_____

b. _____

_____

Practice 2: Worship—Building community and hope

Effective rural congregations provide vital worship experiences that celebrate the mystery of the extraordinary in the midst of the ordinary; cast a vision of hope and meaningful discipleship; sometimes even in the face of hopelessness; and build a sense of family and community in places where there can be loneliness and isolation.

1. Key insights concerning this practice include:

_____

_____

_____

2. The two action steps identified are:

a. _____

_____

b. _____

_____

Practice 3: Making Disciples—Learning to live Jesus' way

Effective rural congregations encourage people to join the adventure and journey of discipleship by creating a culture that centers on Bible study and devotional reflection. Learning to follow Jesus with one's whole heart, mind, and body is the aim. Their teaching focus, while certainly content based, aims more at equipping adults, youth, and children to live a lifestyle that is Christ's style.

1. Key insights concerning this practice include:

_____

_____

_____

2. The two action steps identified are:

a. _____

_____

b. _____

_____

Practice 4: Evangelism—A way of life

Effective rural congregations exhibit a wholistic approach to evangelism built on relationship, centered on events, and focused on meeting the specific needs of people in their community.

1. Key insights concerning this practice include:

_____

_____

_____

2. The two action steps identified are:

a. _____

_____

b. _____

_____

Practice 5: Caring Ministries—Serving as Jesus served

Effective rural congregations make Christ known and develop positive, attractive reputations by stepping out into their neighborhood and world through acts of caring service and social ministry. This social outreach is a natural expression of their discipleship and an ingredient within the mix that contributes to their vitality and spiritual energy.

1. Key insights concerning this practice include:

_____

_____

_____

2. The two action steps identified are:

a. _____

_____

b. _____

_____

Practice 6: Leadership—Who's driving the tractor?

Effective rural congregations model a shared leadership in which the pastor's role is significant yet not dominant, the role of the laity is active rather than passive, and Jesus is seen as the primary leader all in the congregation follow.

1. Key insights concerning this practice include:

_____

_____

_____

2. The two action steps identified are:

a. _____

_____

b. _____

_____

Context: The gift of your place

Effective rural congregations celebrate and leverage the unique gifts of their place and people.

  1. Key insights concerning this practice include:

  _____

  _____

  _____

  2. Ministry opportunities that emerge from the questions at the end of chapter 8 include:

  _____

  _____

  _____

Moving into God's preferred future

Review the information you've captured on this questionnaire. Now comes the hard part. What is God calling your congregation to be and do as a result of this learning? Take some time to develop an action plan that is SMART (Specific, Measurable, Attainable, Realistic, and Timely). You cannot do everything. Together, discern what your highest priorities are at the time. Then determine the tasks involved, when they need to be done, and who will be responsible for implementation.

Going Deeper: Resources for Further Study

Rural and General Ministry

Avery, William O. *Cooperating Congregations: Portraits of Mission Strategies.* Alban Institute, 2000.

Bierly, Steve R. *Help for the Small-Church Pastor: Unlocking the Potential of Your Congregation.* Zondervan Publishing, 1995.

Coote, Robert B., ed. *Mustard-Seed Churches: Ministries in Small Churches.* Fortress Press, 1990.

Crandall, Ron. *Turnaround Strategies for the Small Church.* Abingdon Press, 1995.

Farris, Lawrence W., and Norma Cook Everist. *Dynamics of Small Town Ministry.* Alban Institute, 2000.

Jung, L. Shannon, et al. *Rural Ministry: The Shape of the Renewal to Come.* Abingdon Press, 1998.

Jung, Shannon, and Mary A. Agria. *Rural Congregational Studies: A Guide for Good Shepherds.* Abingdon Press, 1997.

Jung, L. Shannon, and Russ May. *Transforming Congregations: Leadership Practices That Form Communities for Mission.* Center for Theology and Land (monograph).

Klassen, Ron. *No Little Places: The Untapped Potential of the Small-Town Church.* Baker Book House, 1997.

Lofy, Chuck. *A Grain of Wheat: Giving Voice to the Spirit of Change.* Changing Church, 1993.

Ruffcorn, Kevin E. *Rural Evangelism: Catching the Vision.* Augsburg Fortress, 1994.

Schmitmeyer, James. *A Calendar of Care: Reflections of a Country Pastor.* Liturgy Training Publications, 1999.

Schwarz, Christian A. *Natural Church Development: A Guide to Eight Essential Qualities of Healthy Churches.* ChurchSmart Resources, 1998.

Videos for rural ministry

Renewed: Reinventing Rural Ministry. 91 minutes. ELCA Division for Congregational Ministries, 1995.

Renewed: Renewing Rural Ministry. 30 minutes. ELCA Division for Congregational Ministries, 1995.

Prayer

Dahlseng, Brent. *Growing Your Congregation's Prayer Ministries: A Key to Strengthening Evangelism and Discipleship in Your Setting.* ELCA Division for Congregational Ministries, 1998.

Foster, Richard J. *Prayer: Finding the Heart's True Home.* HarperCollins. 1992.

Griend, Vander. *The Praying Church Sourcebook.* Church Development Resources, 1997.

Murray, Andrew. *With Christ in the School of Prayer.* Bridge-Logos, 1999.

Petersen, Bjorn. *Face to Face with God in Your Church: Establishing a Prayer Ministry.* Augsburg Fortress, 1995.

Worship

Hoff, Judy F. *Psalms from the Heartland.* St. Mary's Press, 1995.

McCarthy, Scott. *Celebrating the Earth: An Earth-Centered Theology of Worship with Blessings, Prayers, and Rituals.* Resource Publications, 1992.

Newman, Toni L., ed. *Worship from the Ground Up: A Worship Resource for Town and Country Congregations.* The Center for Theology and Land (monograph).

Discipleship and Christian education

Living Faith: Call to Discipleship (planning guide). Evangelical Lutheran Church in America and Augsburg Fortress, 2000. (For more information, visit www.elca.org/init/teachthefaith.)

Foss, Michael. *Power Surge: Six Marks of Discipleship for a Changing Church.* Augsburg Fortress, 2000.

Foster, Richard. *Celebration of Discipline: The Path to Spiritual Growth.* HarperCollins, 1988.

Ogden, Greg. *Discipleship Essentials: A Guide to Building Your Life in Christ.* InterVarsity Press, 1998.

Evangelism

Friendship Sunday Planning Guide. ELCA, 1994.

Sharing Faith in Daily Life: A Small Group Study. ELCA, 1999.

Poling-Goldenne, David, et al. *Making Christ Known: A Guide to Evangelism for Congregations.* Augsburg Fortress, 1996.

Videos for evangelism

Faith! Living It, Sharing It (video workshop). ELCA, 1999.

Go Public! Communication Evangelism (video workshop and workbook). Augsburg Fortress, 1997.

Making Christ Known: Outreach to Go (video workshop). ELCA, 2001.

Caring ministries

Ishida, Emily Demuth, and Y. Franklin Ishida. *To Serve as Jesus Served: A Guide to Social Ministry for Congregations.* Augsburg Fortress, 1994.

Kysar, Robert D. *Called To Care: Biblical Images for Social Ministry.* Fortress Press, 1991.

Leadership

Ford, Leighton. *Transforming Leadership: Jesus' Way of Creating Vision, Shaping Values and Empowering Change.* Inter Varsity Press, 1991.

Jones, Laurie Beth. *Jesus CEO: Using Ancient Wisdom for Visionary Leadership.* Hyperion, 1995.

Kallestad, Walt. *The Everyday, Anytime Guide to Christian Leadership.* Augsburg Fortress, 1994.

APPENDIX

Research Procedures and Participants

This research study was initiated by the Evangelical Lutheran Church in America (ELCA) Division for Congregational Ministries and Division for Outreach, in partnership with the Center for Theology and Land at Wartburg Seminary in Dubuque, Iowa, and funded through a generous grant from the Lutheran Brotherhood Foundation. Other significant participants included the ELCA Department for Research and Evaluation and Augsburg Fortress, Publishers.

The purpose of this study was to learn the best practices from exemplary ELCA small-town and rural congregations in terms of evangelism, Christian education, and leadership development in order to uncover replicable models, principles, and ideas for "what works" in this particular context for ministry.

Letters were sent to judicatory and rural network leaders throughout the 65 synods of the ELCA. These leaders were invited to nominate up to three congregations within their synod or ministry area that fit the following profile:

"Rural and small-town congregations, of varying sizes and settings, that have committed themselves to evangelism, outreach, and spiritual growth, and are experiencing congregational transformation because of that commitment." More than 160 congregations were nominated from all across the United States.

At the same time, a statistical search was conducted on the more than 5,000 ELCA congregations in rural and small town contexts. This search, based on a variety of growth and vitality parameters, was conducted with the ELCA Department for Research and Evaluation and its extensive database on congregations.

When the nomination list was compared to feedback from the statistical search, 140 congregations were identified as candidates for the research study in the autumn of 1998. These 140 congregations received letters inviting them to consider participating in further study. Along with an explanation of the project and the nomination process, congregations received an extensive questionnaire for the pastor and three questionnaires for lay leaders to complete. The congregations were asked to return completed questionnaires in order to be considered for the next phase of the study. Forty-nine congregations responded to this invitation.

The leadership team read all of the questionnaires and selected 26 congregations to continue on in the study. These selections were based on a process of prayer and discernment, and a commitment to select congregations representing a variety of rural settings and locations in this country.

Over a three-month period in 1999, these 26 congregations were invited to convene on-site "discovery teams" of up to 10 people representing the diversity of their congregation. These teams met two or three times to discuss and complete comprehensive "Discovery Guides" to help them fully share their congregation's history, context, and ministry practices.

The 26 completed Discovery Guides were then studied by all members of the leadership team. During a two-day meeting, the team drafted a list of the characteristics and practices that appeared to be keys to congregational vitality in rural settings. This list was then tested during the next phase of the study.

In September 1999, each of the 26 congregations was invited to select three people (a pastor and two lay leaders) to attend a three-day Discovery Event for a "mega focus group" session. Nine smaller focus groups were formed by grouping congregations from similar contexts together. Through these focus groups and large group listening sessions, invited presentations, and a variety of other exercises designed to elicit sharing of best practices, a wealth of information was captured on audiotape and computer. Members of the leadership team studied this information, then met in February 2000, to identify and summarize key insights and develop outlines for print and video resources.

The research this book exemplifies is narrative research based on stories and insights gleaned from effective congregations. This information is not statistically quantifiable research (as opposed to purely statistical or mathematical research). Also, it was clear to the leadership team throughout this study that there were dozens of other congregations that could have been part of the research pool. Although invitations were broadly extended, the fact of the matter is that the leadership team worked with the congregations that responded. Obviously, there are other congregations that could have been on the initial list of 140 and there are certainly congregations within this list that may have been too busy or too engaged to have time to respond.

The 26 congregations, their context, and representatives

California

Sierra Lutheran, Auberry: A rural foothills ranching and logging community with growing identity as a bedroom community of Fresno; 16 years in ministry; Rev. Mark A. Bankson, Chris Cunningham.

Colorado

Christ the King Lutheran, Durango: A town setting with tourism and recreation as a focus and a growing population of computer-based telecommuters: more than 25 years in ministry; Rev. John E. Knutson, Diane Knutson, Harold Steinhoff, John Welcher.

Florida

Christ the King Lutheran, Sebastian: A rural fishing village with an economy based on health, education, and recreation; 15 years in ministry; Rev. Paul E. Hauenstein, Evelyn Heden, Frank Deloach, Elizabeth Clark.

Idaho

Grace Lutheran, Mountain Home: Originally a stagecoach stop on the Oregon Trail, now a rural agriculture and Air Force community; more than 20 years in ministry; Rev. Philip A. Yonkers, Carmen Metzer, Laurice Bentz.

Illinois

Immanuel Lutheran, Amboy: An agriculture and manufacturing town setting; more than 130 years in ministry; Rev. Christine Stienstra, Craig Watkins, Cliff Weller.

Iowa

St. John Lutheran, Nashua: A rural town context that serves as a bedroom community to neighboring towns; more than 100 years in ministry; Revs. David and Joann Kramer, Tracy Wiebke, Cheryl Gerdes.

Massachusetts

Bethlehem Lutheran, Sturbridge: A historical farm community with tourism as its present primary focus; more than 15 years in ministry; Rev. Julie B. Bergdahl, Nancy Colangione, Linda Gauthier.

Minnesota

Maynard-Wang Lutheran, Maynard: A two-point rural parish in a rural farming and small manufacturing context; more than 100 years of ministry for both congregations; Rev. Mary L. Hovland, Jackie Ast, Kathy Hendrickson.

Zion Lutheran Church of Amor, Battle Lake: A rural bedroom, retirement, and recreation context with the church as a focal point;

more than 120 years in ministry; Rev. Jim Gronbeck, Kerri McFarland, Laverne Nelson.

Montana

Christ Lutheran, Whitefish: A small town, lumber community transitioning to tourism, recreation, and telecommuting; more than 75 years in ministry; Rev. John C. Bent, Marcia Malmi, Jeffrey Scogin, Jeff Teeples.

Nebraska

Trinity Lutheran, Paxton: A town setting with agriculture as the primary focus and some manufacturing; 100 years in ministry; Rev. Doniver Peterson, Joann Baumeister, Kathy Leirley.

New York

St. Andrew Lutheran, South Glen Falls: A rural regional congregation in a health care, corridor context; more than 10 years in ministry; Rev. Stephen C. Biegner, Tim Syrell, Rudi Bowin-Smith.

St. Peter's Lutheran, Verona: A town in transition from farming roots to a more mobile and diverse community; more than 160 years in ministry, transitioned to a new site and building in 1995; Rev. Bradley J. Hales, Richard Warner, Douglas Bailey.

Zion Lutheran, Cobleskill: A two point rural parish; town congregation is the focal point in a service oriented rural context; more than 200 years in ministry; Rev. John Seltzer, Mara Kerr, Sandy Shear.

North Dakota

Fordville Lutheran, Fordville: A small town where the grain elevator is still the focal symbol and the congregation's pastor is the one resident clergy; more than 100 years in ministry; Rev. Corey Bjertness, Beverly Bjertness, Carla Helland.

Portland Parish, Portland: A cooperative ministry representing six congregations (four country and two town settings) with two pastors, an associate in ministry, and a parish administrator; serving a large geographical area with agriculture as the primary focus; Rev. Eric J. Hultstrand, Brad Thykeson, Jim Lambert.

Pennsylvania

Zion Lutheran, Zion Hill: Small rural village of 60 homes with some retail and manufacturing; 160 years in ministry; Rev. James R. Saboe, Richard Ottinger, Terry Ottinger.

South Dakota

East Lake Andes Lutheran, Lake Andes: Open-country congregation with agriculture as the primary occupation; more than 100 years in ministry; Rev. Nancy Nyland, Karen Weber, Lea Yumker.

Texas

Trinity Lutheran, Blanco: A transitioning small town becoming a bedroom community to San Antonio and Austin with recreation and service industry as the main focus; 95 years in ministry; Rev. Anamae S. Storbeck, Bill Mikeska, Nina Artz.

Virginia

Bethel Lutheran, Winchester: A town setting with a base in agriculture, health care, and education; more than 180 years in ministry; Rev. D. Rhodes Woolly, David Shoberg, Jane McAllister.

Washington

Immanuel Lutheran, Everson: A transitioning rural farming and logging community, now also a bedroom community; 110 years in ministry; Rev. Stan Jacobsen, Linda Anderson, Jeff Curtis.

Wisconsin

Salem Lutheran, Shell Lake: Small town without a single stoplight; local government seat; logging, farming, service economy; more than 110 years in ministry; Revs. Laurie and Tom Engesser, Lois Eichman, Darrell Aderman.

Trinity Lutheran, Spooner: Large town service center and vacation destination area; more than 50 years in ministry; Revs. Will and Carolyn Mowchan, Fred Krueger, Sue Donatell.

Cross Lutheran, Ixonia: Farming community with a mill as its focal point and an increasing number of commuters to Milwaukee and Madison; more than 125 years in ministry; Rev. Laurie Stumme-Diers, Mary Frankiewiez, Dawn Hannula.

Redeemer Lutheran, Plymouth: A rural service town with five cheese processing plants; more than 50 years in ministry; Rev. James A. Wilson Sr., Denise Wilson, Karen Smith.

Wyoming

St. Luke's Lutheran, Buffalo: Small town with an agricultural, mining, logging, and recreation focus; 80 years in ministry; Rev. Kim Wilker, Dolores Meier, Cathy Trabing.

Members of the Research Leadership Team

Cindy Cone, Cherokee, Iowa, representing the Great Plain's Coalition.

Leonard Dale, Shawnee Mission, Kansas, representing the ELCA Small Town and Rural (STaR) Team.

Barbara Holzhauser, Salem, Ohio, Project Director.

L. Shannon Jung, Dubuque, Iowa, representing the Center for Theology and Land, Wartburg Seminary.

Sandra A. La Blanc, Des Moines, Iowa, ELCA Director for Rural Ministry.

Carolyn Mowchan, Spooner, Wisconsin, representing the ELCA Synodical Evangelism Network.

David Poling-Goldenne, Chicago, Illinois, representing the ELCA Division for Congregational Ministries, Project Leader.

Andrea Lee Schieber, Minneapolis, Minnesota, representing Augsburg Fortress, Publishers.

Martin Smith, Chicago, Illinois, representing the ELCA Department for Research and Evaluation.

Warren Sorteberg, Chicago, Illinois, representing the ELCA Division for Outreach.